# INTRODUCTION

There is no better way to welcome in the holidays than with a quilt. Whether it's on the wall, a table, a bed or a chair, a festive quilt adds a bit of cozy charm to winter decor. This book includes small projects to make in a day and quilts that take a little more time and planning, so you are sure to find a project that fits your schedule and will allow you to deck the halls.

Add this book to your library and turn to it time and time again for just the right project. Make your list, plan your fabrics and start sewing. It's never too early or late to work on holiday projects!

# TABLE OF CONTENTS

# CHRISTMAS DISHES

Designed & Quilted by Mercedes Rose

Classic Christmas colors of red and green create a quilt that brings a festive and timeless charm to your holiday decor.

## SKILL LEVEL

Confident Beginner

## FINISHED SIZE

Quilt Size: 38" x 38"

## MATERIALS

- 1½ yards red stripe print*
- 1 yard white print*
- ½ yard green stripe print*
- 1½ yards backing*
- 42" x 42" batting
- Thread
- Basic sewing tools and supplies

**Fabrics from the Shimmer Sparkle collection by Deborah Edwards for Northcott Fabrics used to make sample.*

## PROJECT NOTES

Read all instructions before beginning this project.

Stitch right sides together using a ¼" seam allowance unless otherwise specified.

Materials and cutting lists assume 40" of usable fabric width for yardage.

Arrows indicate directions to press seams.

WOF – width of fabric
HST – half-square triangle ⧅
QST – quarter-square triangle ⊠

## CUTTING

### FROM RED STRIPE PRINT CUT:

- 14 (5½") B squares
- 12 (5") D squares
- 5 (2½" x WOF) binding strips
- 2 (1½" x 38") F border strips
- 2 (1½" x 36") E border strips

### FROM WHITE PRINT CUT:

- 26 (5½") A squares

### FROM GREEN STRIPE PRINT CUT:

- 12 (5½") C squares

## COMPLETING THE HALF-SQUARE TRIANGLE UNITS

**1.** Refer to Half-Square Triangles on page 37 to make two A-B units using one each A and B square (Figure 1a). Trim the units to 5" x 5". Make 28.

**2.** Repeat step 1 to make 24 A-C units using 12 each A and C squares (Figure 1b).

a. A-B Unit Make 28

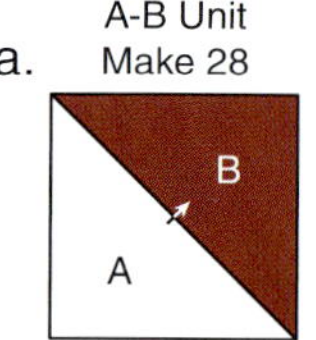


b. A-C Unit Make 24

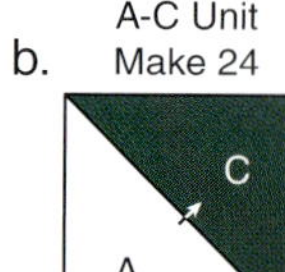


**Figure 1**

## Here's a Tip

*When making half-square triangle units using stripe fabric, it can be tricky to have the stripes run in the same direction throughout the design. Make half of the units with the stripe direction vertical and the other half with the stripe direction horizontal to yield an equal number of units that can be rotated as needed to keep the stripes consistent.*

## Inspiration

*"This quilt was inspired by the broken dishes block. I was playing around with the block on my EQ8 program and this was the result."* —*Mercedes Rose*

## COMPLETING THE QUILT

**1.** Referring to the Assembly Diagram, arrange the A-B units, A-C units and D squares in eight rows. Sew into rows, then sew the rows together to complete the quilt center.

**2.** Sew the E border strips to the sides of the quilt center and the F border strips to the top and bottom to complete the quilt top.

**3.** Layer, baste, quilt as desired and bind referring to Quilting Basics. The photographed quilt was quilted with diagonal lines. ■

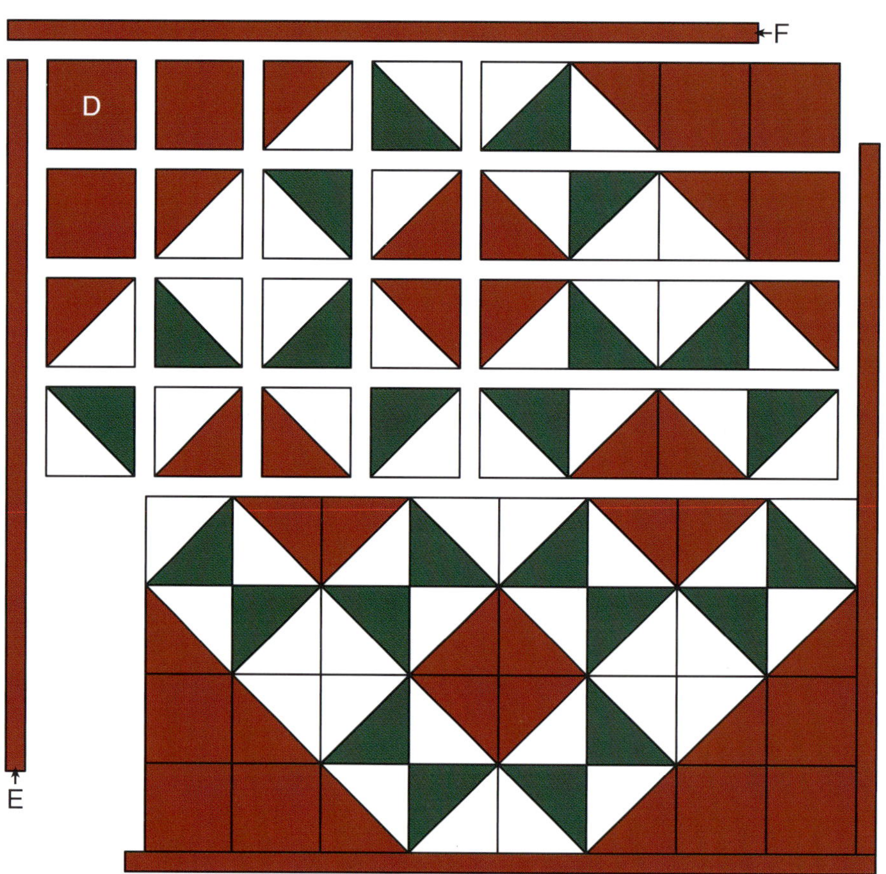


**Christmas Dishes**
Assembly Diagram 38" x 38"

# MISTLETOE & MINT

Designed & Quilted by Jill Metzger

Two creative blocks on a frosty white background, sashing and a pieced border make a great quilt to snuggle under throughout the holiday season.

## SKILL LEVEL

Confident Beginner

## FINISHED SIZES

Quilt Size: 66" x 81¾"

Block Sizes: 12" x 12", 6" x 6" and 3¾" x 3¾"

Number of Blocks: 12, 22 and 20

## MATERIALS

- 4¾ yards off-white solid*
- 2 yards red plaid*
- 1 yard each forest green, medium olive green and red prints*
- ½ yard olive green print*
- ¾ yard binding plaid*
- 5¼ yards backing*
- 74" x 90" batting*
- Thread
- Basic sewing tools and supplies

**Fabrics from the Christmas Is In Town collection by Sandy Gervais and Confetti Cottons for Riley Blake Designs; Warm & Natural Cotton batting from the Warm Company used to make sample.*

## PROJECT NOTES

Read all instructions before beginning this project.

Stitch right sides together using a ¼" seam allowance unless otherwise specified.

Materials and cutting lists assume 40" of usable fabric width for yardage.

Arrows indicate directions to press seams.

WOF – width of fabric
HST – half-square triangle ⧅
QST – quarter-square triangle ⊠

## CUTTING

### FROM OFF-WHITE SOLID CUT:

- 3 (8") L squares
- 12 (7¼") I squares, then cut once diagonally ⧅
- 12 (6½" x 7⅛") T rectangles
- 10 (6½") U squares
- 11 (6") N squares
- 24 (3½") A squares
- 48 (2½") B squares
- 3 (2" x WOF) C strips
- 26 (1¾" x WOF) R strips
- 48 (1½" x 3½") D rectangles

**Mistletoe**
12" x 12" Finished Block
Make 6

**Mint**
12" x 12" Finished Block
Make 6

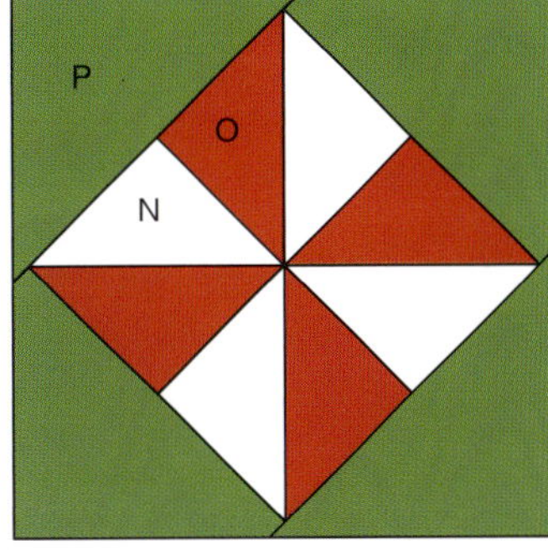


**Peppermint**
6" x 6" Finished Block
Make 22

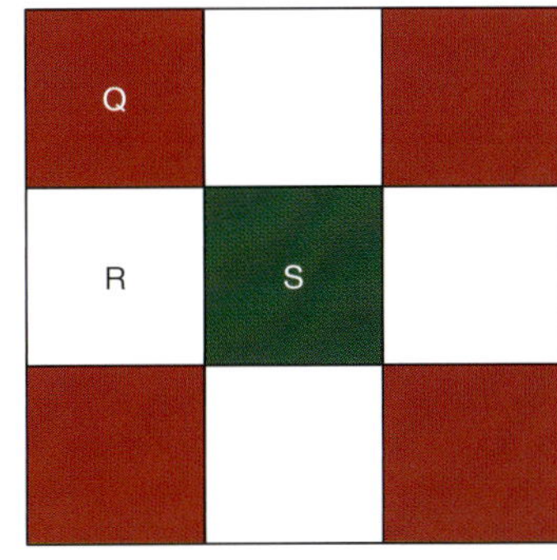


**Nine-Patch**
3¾" x 3¾" Finished Block
Make 20

### FROM RED PLAID CUT:

- 3 (8") M squares
- 24 (2½") J squares
- 7 (2" x WOF) strips, stitch short ends to short ends, then subcut into:
  2 (2" x 67¼") V and 2 (2" x 54½") W border strips
- 3 (2" x WOF) G strips
- 15 (1¾" x WOF) Q strips
- 24 (1½") H squares

### FROM FOREST GREEN PRINT CUT:

- 48 (2½" x 3½") E rectangles
- 48 (2½") F squares
- 1 (1¾" x WOF) S strip

### FROM MEDIUM OLIVE GREEN PRINT CUT:

- 44 (4¾") P squares, then cut once diagonally

### FROM RED PRINT CUT:

- 11 (6") O squares

### FROM OLIVE GREEN PRINT CUT:

- 12 (5½") K squares, then cut once diagonally

### FROM BINDING PLAID CUT:

- 8 (2½" x WOF) binding strips

## COMPLETING THE BLOCKS

### MISTLETOE

**1.** Sew one each C and G strip together lengthwise to make a strip set. Make three. Cut 48 (2" x 3½") C-G units from strip sets (Figure 1).

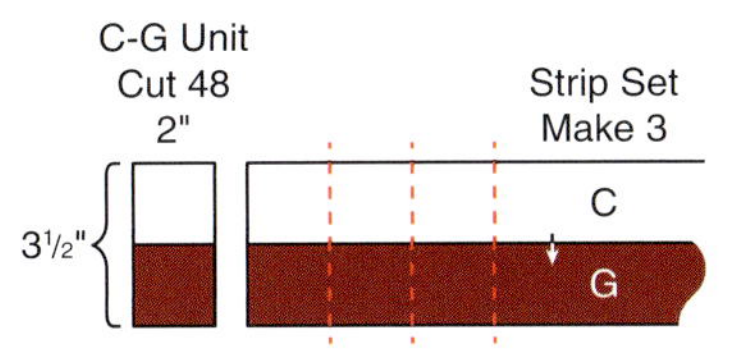


Figure 1

**2.** Noting fabric orientation, sew two C-G units together to make one corner section (Figure 2). Make 24.

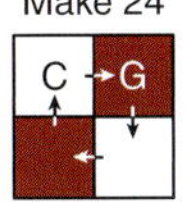


Figure 2

## Here's a Tip

*Spin four-patch seams to remove seam allowance bulk and create flatter blocks. Refer to Spinning Centers to Reduce Bulk on page 10 to make the seams rotate around the center point.*

**3.** Refer to Sew & Flip Corners to add a corner triangle on the upper right corner of one E rectangle using a B square to complete one left B-E unit (Figure 3a). Repeat but place B on the upper left corner of E to make a right B-E unit (Figure 3b). Make 24 of each.

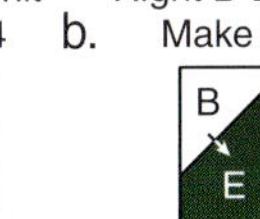


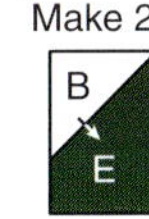


Figure 3

**4.** Noting fabric orientation, sew a left B-E unit to the left of one right B-E unit, then sew a D rectangle to each side to complete one side section (Figure 4). Make 24.

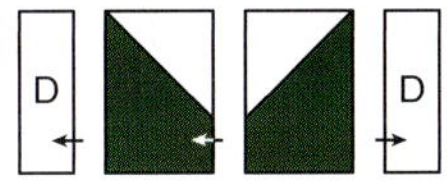


Figure 4

## SEW & FLIP CORNERS

Use this method to add triangle corners in a quilt block.

**1.** Draw a diagonal line from corner to corner on the wrong side of the specified square. Place the square, right sides together, on the indicated corner of the larger piece, making sure the line is oriented in the correct direction indicated by the pattern (Figure 1).

**2.** Sew on the drawn line. Trim ¼" away from sewn line (Figure 2).

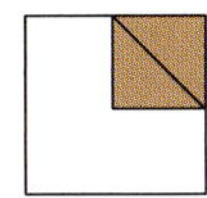

Figure 1

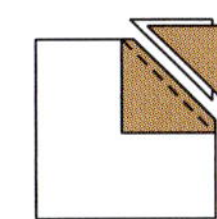

Figure 2

**3.** Open and press to reveal the corner triangle (Figure 3).

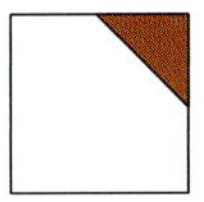

Figure 3

**4.** If desired, square up the finished unit to the required unfinished size. ●

**5.** Refer again to Sew & Flip Corners to add corner triangles on the upper right corner and lower left corner of one A square using two F squares. Then add a corner triangle on the lower right corner of A using one H square to complete one A-F-H unit (Figure 5). Make 24.

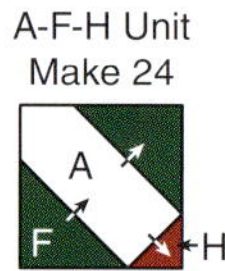


**Figure 5**

**6.** Noting fabric orientation, arrange four A-F-H units in two rows. Sew into rows, then sew the rows together to complete one center section (Figure 6). Make six.

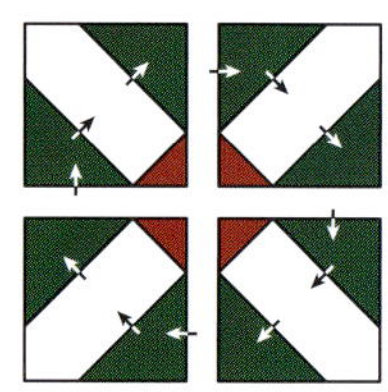

Center Section
Make 6

F
A
H

**Figure 6**

**7.** Arrange one center section and four each corner sections and side sections in three rows. Sew into rows, then sew the rows together to complete one Mistletoe block (Figure 7). Make six.

**Figure 7**

## MINT

**1.** Refer to Eight-at-a-Time Half-Square Triangles to make eight L-M units using one each L and M square (Figure 8a). Trim the units to 3½" x 3½". Make 24.

**2.** Noting fabric orientation, arrange four L-M units in two rows. Sew into rows, then sew the rows together to complete one L-M pinwheel unit (Figure 8b). Make six.

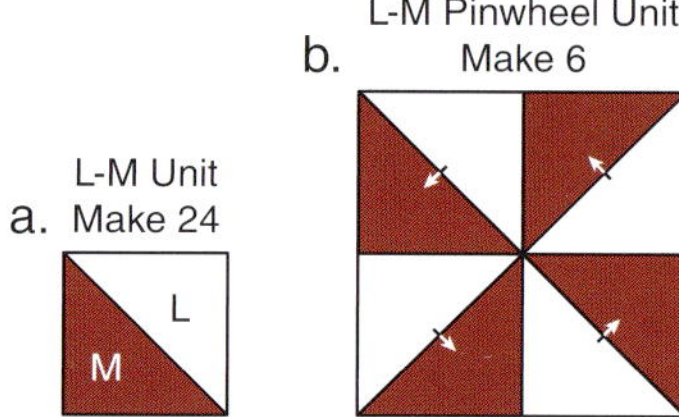


**Figure 8**

# EIGHT-AT-A-TIME HALF-SQUARE TRIANGLES

Half-square triangles (HSTs) are a basic unit of quilting used in many blocks or on their own. This construction method will yield eight HST units.

**1.** Refer to the pattern for size to cut squares. The standard formula is to add 1" to the finished size of the square then multiply by 2. Cut two squares from different colors this size. For example, for a 3" finished HST unit, cut 8" squares (3" + 1" = 4"; 4" x 2 = 8").

**2.** Draw two diagonal lines from corner to corner on the wrong side of the lightest color square. Layer the squares right sides together. Stitch ¼" on either side of both drawn lines (Figure A).

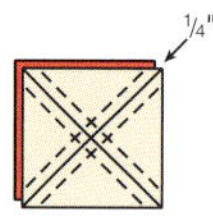


**Figure A**

**3.** Cut the sewn squares in half horizontally and vertically, making four squares. Then cut each square apart on the drawn line, leaving a ¼" seam allowance and making eight HST units referring to Figure B. Trim each HST unit to the desired size (3½" in this example).

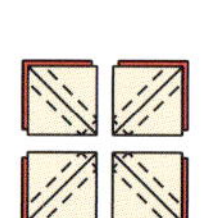

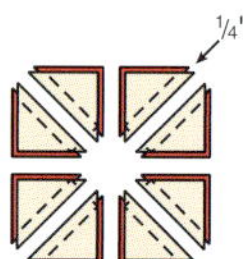


**Figure B**

**4.** Open the HST units and press seam allowances toward the darker fabric making eight HST units (Figure C). ●

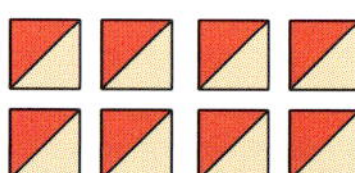

**Figure C**

**3.** Position the long edge of one K triangle centered on one side of an L-M pinwheel unit; sew together. Repeat on the opposite side, then again on the two remaining sides (Figure 9). Trim the unit to 9" x 9", keeping the design centered. Make six.

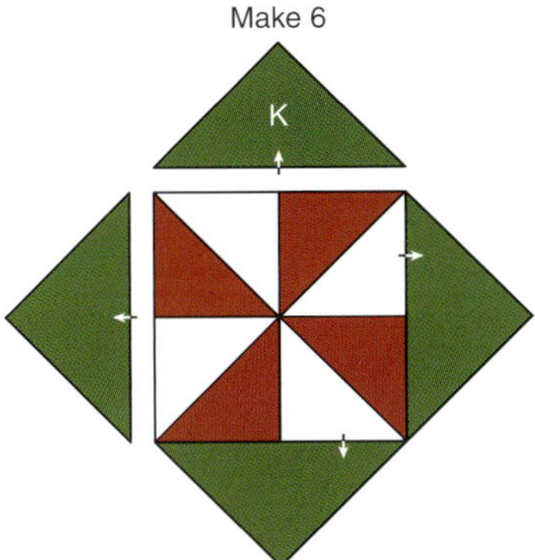


**Figure 9**

**4.** Position the long edge of one I triangle centered on one side of a step 3 unit; sew together. Repeat on the opposite side, then again on the two remaining sides (Figure 10). Trim the unit to 12½" x 12½", keeping the design centered. Make six.

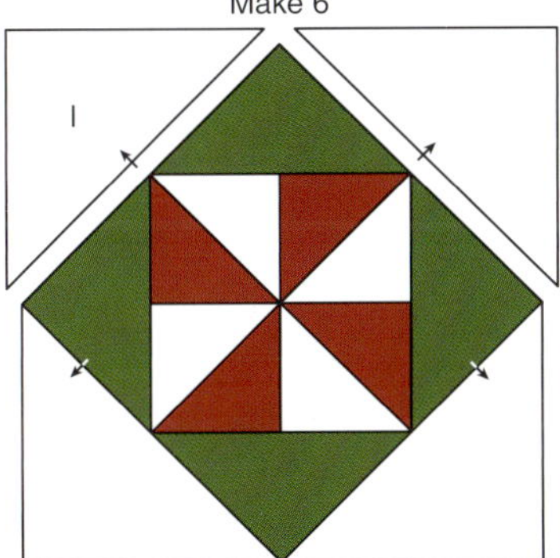


**Figure 10**

**5.** Refer again to Sew & Flip Corners to add corner triangles on all four corners of one step 4 unit using four J squares to complete one Mint block (Figure 11). Make six.

**Figure 11**

## PEPPERMINT

**1.** Refer again to Eight-at-a-Time Half-Square Triangles to make eight N-O units using one each N and O square (Figure 12a). Trim the units to 2½" x 2½". Make 88.

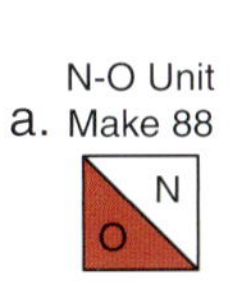


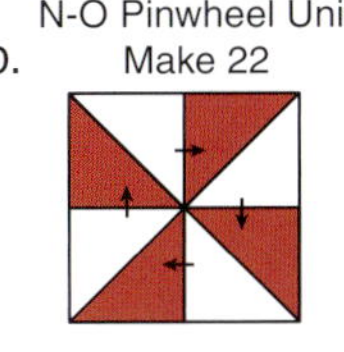


**Figure 12**

**2.** Noting fabric orientation, arrange four N-O units in two rows. Sew into rows, then sew the rows together to complete one N-O pinwheel unit (Figure 12b). Make 22.

**3.** Position the long edge of one P triangle centered on one side of an N-O pinwheel unit; sew together. Repeat on the opposite side, then again on the two remaining sides (Figure 13). Trim the unit to 6½" x 6½", keeping the design centered, to complete one Peppermint block. ***Note:*** *The corners of the pinwheel do not touch the edge of the trimmed block; the trimmed P triangles are larger than the pinwheel.* Make 22.



**Figure 13**

## NINE-PATCH

**1.** Sew one Q strip to each long side of an R strip to make a strip set. Make two. Cut 40 (1¾" x 4¼") Q-R-Q units from the strip sets (Figure 14).

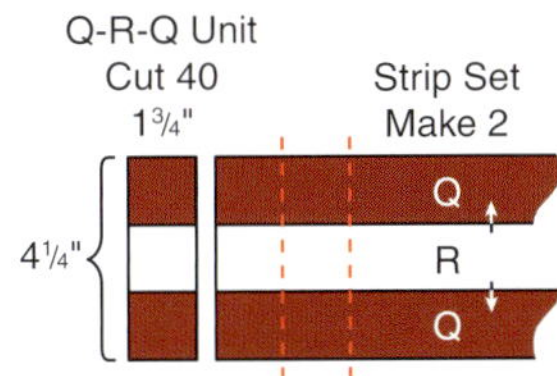


**Figure 14**

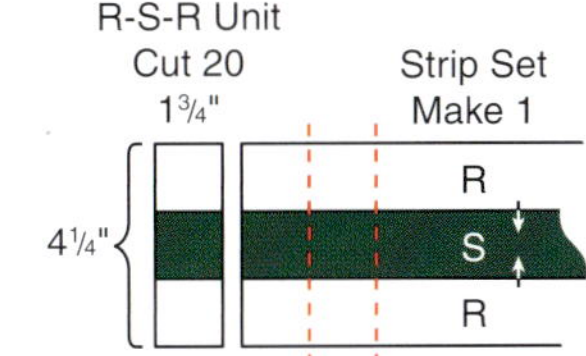


**Figure 15**

**2.** Sew one R strip to each long side of an S strip to make a strip set. Cut 20 (1¾" x 4¼") R-S-R units from the strip set (Figure 15).

**3.** Arrange two Q-R-Q units and one R-S-R unit in three columns and sew together to complete one Nine-Patch block (Figure 16). Make 20.

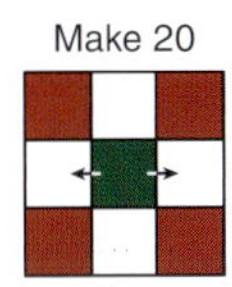


**Figure 16**

## COMPLETING THE SASH UNITS

**1.** Sew one R strip to each long side of a Q strip to make a strip set. Make 11. Cut 31 (12½" x 4¼") sash units from the strip sets (Figure 17).

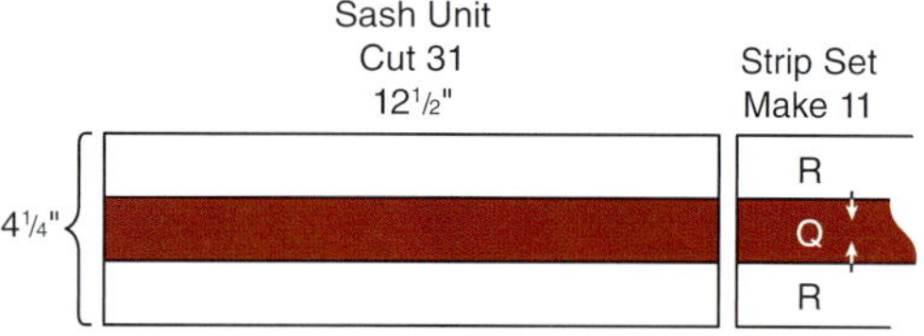


**Figure 17**

## COMPLETING THE PEPPERMINT BORDERS

**1.** Arrange five Peppermint blocks and six T rectangles alternately in a row; sew together to complete one side peppermint border (Figure 18a). Make two.

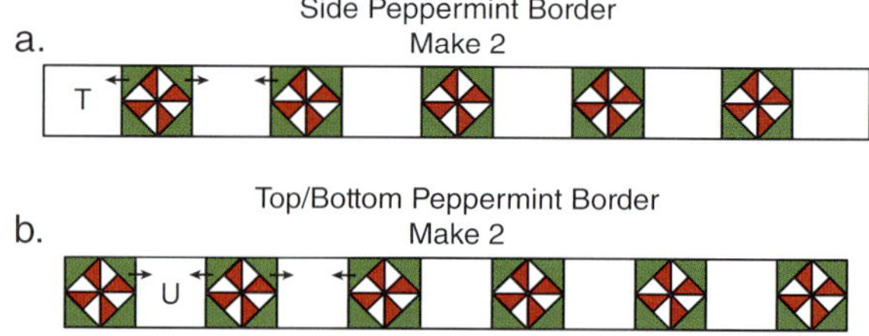


**Figure 18**

**2.** Arrange six Peppermint blocks and five U squares alternately in a row; sew together to complete one top/bottom peppermint border (Figure 18b). Make two.

# SPINNING CENTERS TO REDUCE BULK

When sewing a block where numerous points meet together, there can be a lot of "bulk" in the seam allowance on the wrong side of the fabric. This extra bulk prohibits the block from lying flat when pressed. One option is to trim the points off, thus reducing the amount of fabric in the seam allowance. Another option is to "spin" the center of the seam allowances, thus distributing the bulk more evenly.

**1.** Stitch the block as usual, nesting seams at any intersection (Photo A).

**Photo A**

**2.** Before pressing, remove approximately three stitches in the seam allowance from each side of the previously sewn seams (Photo B).

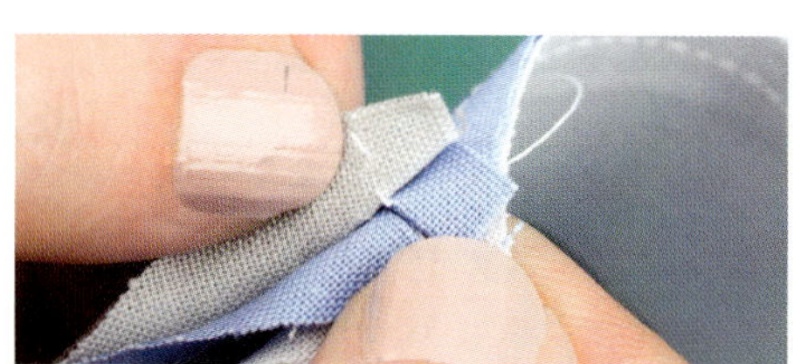

**Photo B**

**3.** Place the block on a pressing board right side down (Photo C).

**Photo C**

**4.** With your finger, push the top seam to the right and the bottom seam to the left (Photo D). This will result in the seam allowances spinning in a clockwise direction.

**Photo D**

**5.** The center will pop open and the seam allowances will swirl around the center of the block. Press with an iron to flatten the seam allowances in place (Photos E and F). ●

**Photo E**

**Photo F**

## COMPLETING THE QUILT

**1.** Referring to the Assembly Diagram, arrange the Mistletoe blocks, Mint blocks, Nine-Patch blocks and sash units alternating in nine rows. Sew into rows, then sew the rows together to complete the quilt center.

**2.** Sew the V border strips to the sides of the quilt center and the W border strips to the top and bottom.

**3.** Sew the side peppermint borders to the sides of the quilt and the top/bottom peppermint borders to the top and bottom to complete the quilt top.

**4.** Stitch around the perimeter of the quilt top, close to the edge, to secure the peppermint border seams.

**5.** Layer, baste, quilt as desired and bind referring to Quilting Basics. The photographed quilt was quilted in-the-ditch around the elements of the design. ■

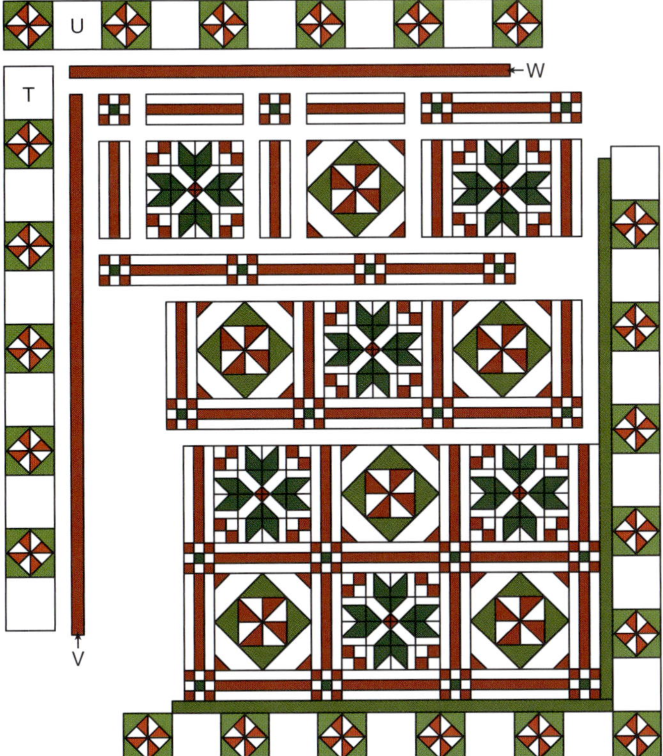


**Mistletoe & Mint**
Assembly Diagram 66" x 81 3/4"

# JOYFUL

Designed & Quilted by Preeti Harris of Sew Preeti Quilts

Try a little free-form piecing to give these sparkling stars individual personalities.

## SKILL LEVEL

Confident Beginner

## FINISHED SIZES

Quilt Size: 51" x 53"

Block Size: 12" x 12"

Number of Blocks: 13

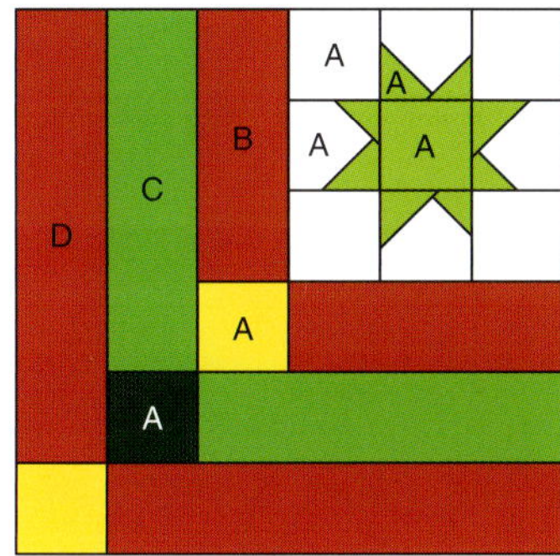


**Log Cabin Star**
12" x 12" Finished Block
Make 13

## MATERIALS

- 2 yards white solid
- ⅓ yard bright red batik
- ¼ yard dark red batik
- ⅓ yard light green batik
- ¼ yard yellow solid
- ¼ yard gray solid
- ⅔ yard assorted green batiks
- ¾ yard assorted red batiks
- 3⅝ yards backing
- 59" x 61" batting*
- Basic sewing tools and supplies

**Thermore® batting from Hobbs Bonded Fibers used to make sample.*

## PROJECT NOTES

Read all instructions before beginning this project.

Stitch right sides together using a ¼" seam allowance unless otherwise specified.

Materials and cutting lists assume 40" of usable fabric width for yardage.

Arrows indicate directions to press seams.

WOF – width of fabric
HST – half-square triangle ⧅
QST – quarter-square triangle ⊠

## CUTTING

### FROM WHITE SOLID CUT:

- 4 (10½") E squares, then cut twice diagonally ⊠
- 2 (10½") F squares, then cut once diagonally ⧅
- 168 (2½") A squares
- 2 (2½" x WOF) strips, then stitch short end to short end to make G border strip
- 6 (2½" x WOF) binding strips

### FROM BRIGHT RED BATIK CUT:

- 8 (2½" x 8½") C rectangles
- 20 (2½") A squares

### FROM DARK RED BATIK CUT:

- 40 (2½") A squares

### FROM LIGHT GREEN BATIK CUT:

- 8 (2½" x 10½") D rectangles
- 8 (2½" x 6½") B rectangles

### FROM YELLOW SOLID CUT:

- 22 (2½") A squares

### FROM GRAY SOLID CUT:

- 17 (2½") A squares

### FROM ASSORTED GREEN BATIKS CUT:

- 9 matching sets of 5 (2½") A squares
- 9 matching sets of 2 (2½" x 8½") C rectangles

### FROM ASSORTED RED BATIKS CUT:

- 9 matching sets of 2 (2½" x 10½") D rectangles and 2 (2½" x 6½") B rectangles

## MAKING THE FREE-FORM STARS

**1.** Select five matching assorted green A squares for your first star. Cut each of four of the squares in half once diagonally. Place a green triangle on a white A square, right sides together, with triangle points overhanging the edges of the white square by about ½" to ¾" (Figure 1). Pin in place and stitch ¼" from the cut edge of the triangle. Press the seam toward the triangle. Repeat the process to add a second triangle to an adjacent corner of the white square; press. Turn the unit over to the wrong side and trim the overhanging edges of the triangles even with the white square. Then trim the corners of the white square leaving ¼" seam allowances. This completes one star point unit. Make four.

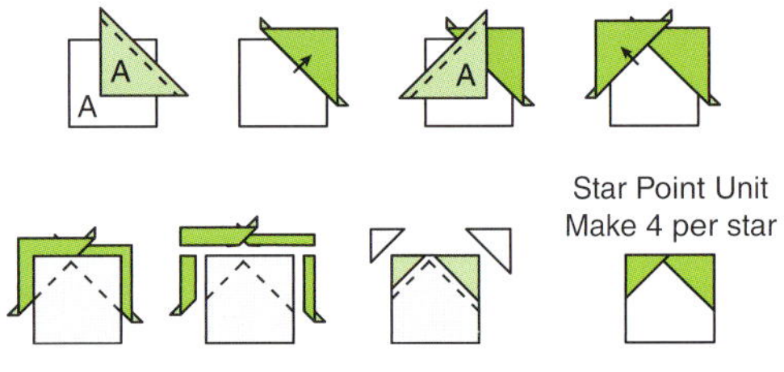


**Figure 1**

**2.** Repeat step 1 to make four matching star point units for each star (nine assorted green, four bright red and eight dark red).

**3.** Using four matching star point units and a matching A square plus four white A squares, arrange and sew three rows of three squares each (Figure 2). Join the rows to complete a star measuring 6½" square from raw edge to raw edge. Make nine assorted green, four bright red and eight dark red stars total.

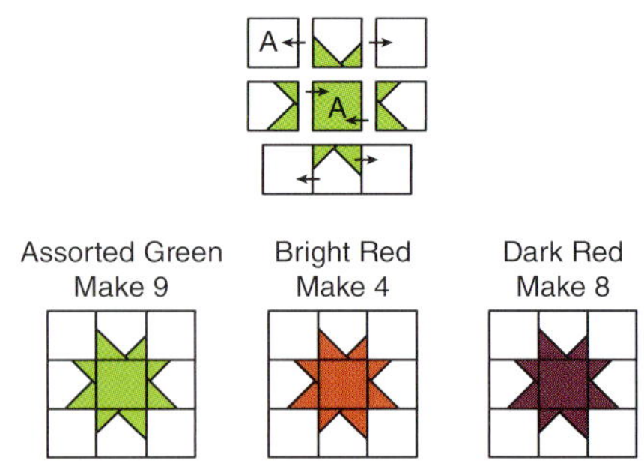


**Figure 2**

## COMPLETING THE BLOCKS & SIDE SETTING TRIANGLES

**1.** Referring to Figure 3, arrange an assorted green star, two each of matching red B and D rectangles, two matching green C rectangles, two yellow A squares and one gray A square as shown. Sew a B rectangle to the bottom of the star. Join the remaining B and a yellow A and sew to the left side of the star. Add a C rectangle to the bottom. Join the remaining C and the gray A and sew to the left side. Sew a D rectangle to the bottom. Join the remaining D and a yellow A and sew to the left side to complete a Log Cabin Star block. Make nine blocks using assorted green stars and four using bright red stars, watching placement of yellow and gray A squares carefully.

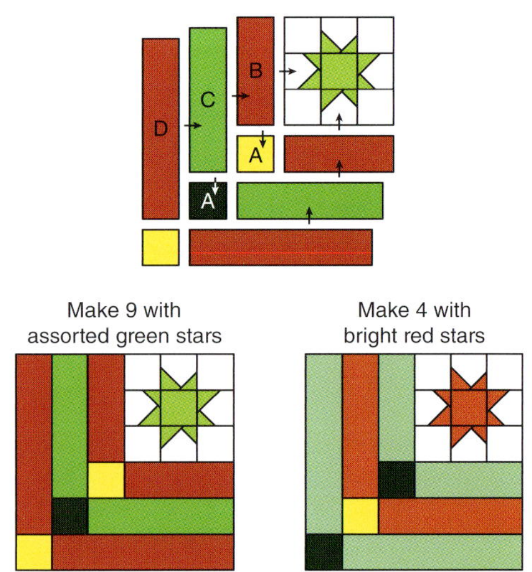


**Figure 3**

**2.** Sew E triangles to adjacent sides of a dark red star to make a side setting triangle (Figure 4). Make eight side setting triangles.

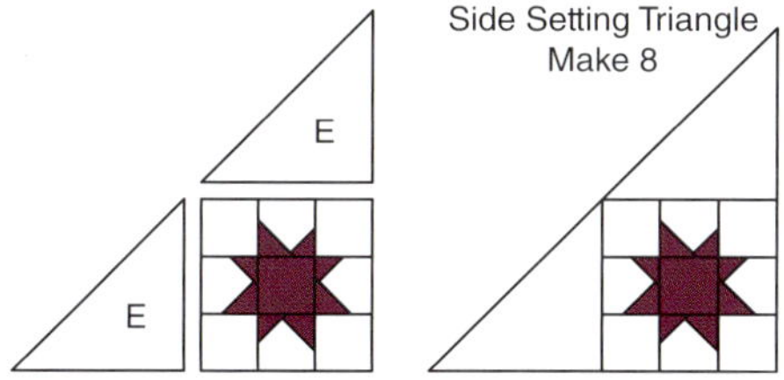


**Figure 4**

## COMPLETING THE QUILT

**1.** Referring to the Assembly Diagram, lay out the blocks in five diagonal rows, noting the placement of the green-star and red-star blocks. Add side setting triangles to the ends of the first, second, fourth and fifth rows as shown.

**2.** Sew the blocks and setting triangles into rows and join the rows. Sew an F triangle to each corner. Press. Trim the quilt edges even at least ¼" outside the outer seam intersections. Make sure to trim corners at right (90-degree) angles.

**3.** Sew the G border strip to the bottom of the quilt top, centering. Trim ends even with the sides of the quilt.

**4.** Layer, baste, quilt as desired and bind referring to Quilting Basics. The photographed quilt was quilted with a wavy diagonal grid. ■

**Joyful**
Assembly Diagram 51" x 53"

## Inspiration

*"This design uses the traditional Old Maid's Puzzle block as its base. My grandmother also used the block in a sampler quilt made many decades ago. I thought it would make a beautiful Christmas quilt." —Megan Dahlinger*

# CHRISTMAS PUZZLE

Design by Megan Dahlinger of Sew Simply Meg Quilts
Quilted by Kristy Mullins of Quilts by Kristy

Traditional blocks in pastel colors create a Christmas quilt with a midcentury modern vibe.

## SKILL LEVEL

Confident Beginner

## FINISHED SIZES

Quilt Size: 52" x 52"
Block Size: 10" x 10"
Number of Blocks: 16

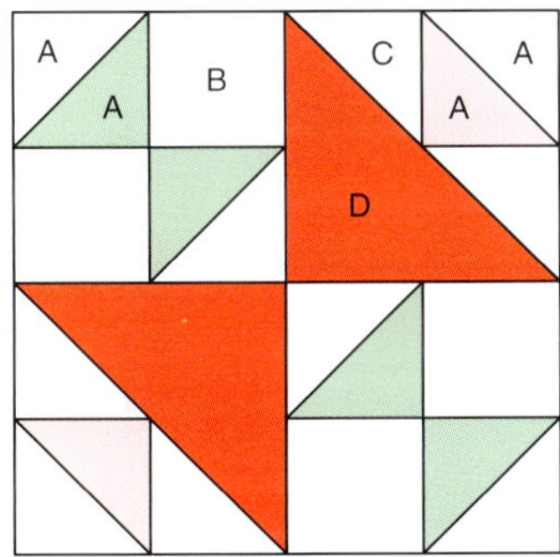


**Christmas Puzzle**
10" x 10" Finished Block
Make 16

## MATERIALS

- 1½ yards cream print
- ½ yard light green print
- ¼ yard pink print
- ⅝ yard red print
- ⅝ yard multicolored print
- ⅝ yard dark green print
- ½ yard binding
- 3⅝ yards backing
- 60" x 60" batting
- Basic sewing tools and supplies

## PROJECT NOTES

Read all instructions before beginning this project.

Stitch right sides together using a ¼" seam allowance unless otherwise specified.

Materials and cutting lists assume 40" of usable fabric width for yardage.

Arrows indicate directions to press seams.

WOF – width of fabric
HST – half-square triangle ◸
QST – quarter-square triangle ⊠

## CUTTING

### FROM CREAM PRINT CUT:

- 12 (7") A squares
- 32 (3⅜") C squares, then cut once diagonally ◸
- 64 (3") B squares

### FROM LIGHT GREEN PRINT CUT:

- 8 (7") A squares

### FROM PINK PRINT CUT:

- 4 (7") A squares

### FROM RED PRINT CUT:

- 16 (5⅞") D squares, then cut once diagonally ◸
- 9 (2½") F squares

### FROM MULTICOLORED PRINT CUT:

- 24 (2½" x 10½") E rectangles

### FROM DARK GREEN PRINT CUT:

- 5 (3½" x WOF) strips, stitch short ends to short ends, then subcut into:
  2 (3½" x 52½") H and 2 (3½" x 46½") G border strips

### FROM BINDING CUT:

- 6 (2½" x WOF) strips

## COMPLETING THE BLOCKS

**1.** Refer to Eight-at-a-Time Half-Square Triangles on page 8 and use the A squares to make 64 HST1 units and 32 HST2 units (Figure 1). Trim all HST units to 3" square, centering the diagonal seam lines.

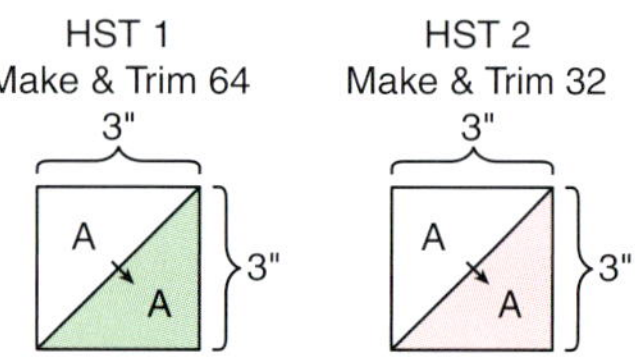


**Figure 1**

### Here's a Tip

*Using the eight-at-a-time half-square triangle (HST) method works perfectly to save time and get exactly the number of HST units needed for all the blocks.*

**2.** Arrange and sew two rows using two HST1 units and two B squares (Figure 2). Join the rows to make an A-B unit measuring 5½" square from raw edge to raw edge. Make 32 A-B units.

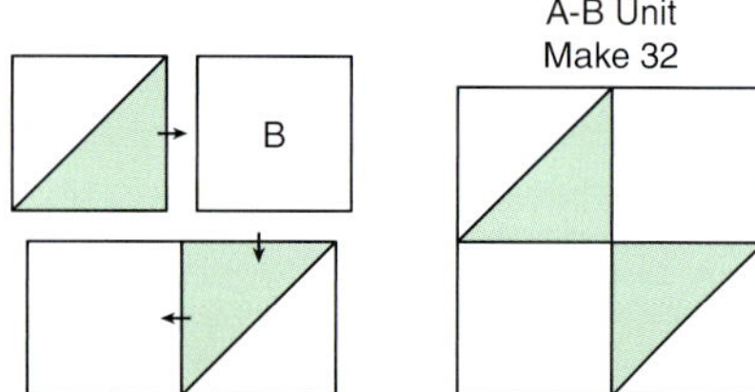


**Figure 2**

**3.** Sew C triangles to the pink sides of an HST2 unit (Figure 3). Add a D triangle to make an A-C-D unit measuring 5½" square. Make 32 A-C-D units.

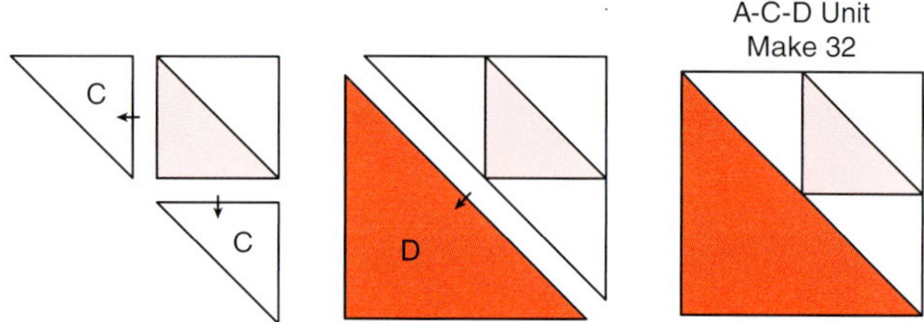


**Figure 3**

**4.** Arrange four units into two rows of two as shown (Figure 4). Sew into rows and join the rows to complete a Christmas Puzzle block. Make 16.

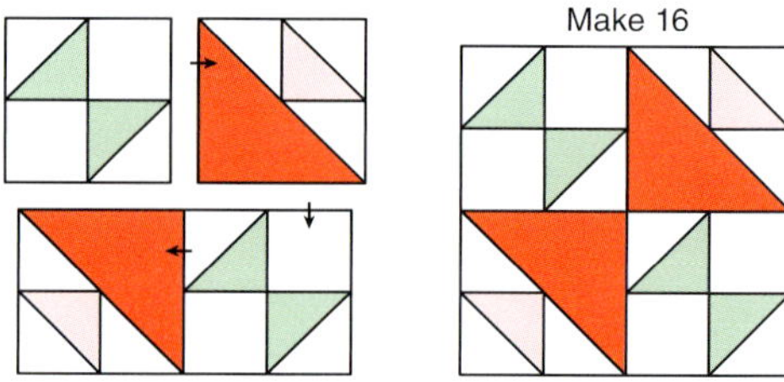


**Figure 4**

## COMPLETING THE QUILT

**1.** Referring to the Assembly Diagram, lay out the blocks in four rows of four blocks each, noting the rotation of the blocks. Add E rectangles and F squares between the blocks as shown.

**2.** Sew the blocks and E rectangles into four block rows. Sew E rectangles and F squares into three sashing rows. Join the rows to complete the quilt center. Press.

**3.** Sew the G and H border strips to the quilt top in alphabetical order.

**4.** Layer, baste, quilt as desired and bind referring to Quilting Basics. The photographed quilt was quilted with the Christmas Doodle pantograph from Urban Elementz. ■

**Christmas Puzzle**
Assembly Diagram 52" x 52"

# LOG CABIN CHRISTMAS

Designed & Quilted by Jen Daly of Jen Daly Quilts

Put a new spin on traditional Log Cabin blocks with cozy Christmas tree centers.

## SKILL LEVEL

Confident Beginner

## FINISHED SIZES

Quilt Size: 70" x 70"

Block Size: 15" x 15"

Number of Blocks: 16

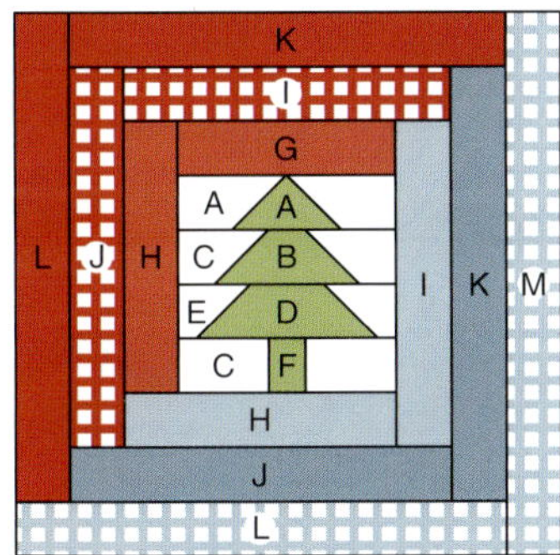


**Log Cabin Tree**
15" x 15" Finished Block
Make 16

## MATERIALS

- 1¼ yards white print*
- ½ yard green print*
- ½ yard red print*
- ⅝ yard blue print*
- ⅔ yard red check*
- ⅔ yard blue snowflake print*
- 1½ yards red snowflake print*
- 1 yard blue check*
- ⅞ yard green check*
- 4⅝ yards backing*
- 78" x 78" batting
- Basic sewing tools and supplies

**Fabrics from the Magical Winterland collection by Lisa Audit for Riley Blake Designs used to make sample. EQ8 was used to design this quilt.*

## PROJECT NOTES

Read all instructions before beginning this project.

Stitch right sides together using a ¼" seam allowance unless otherwise specified.

Materials and cutting lists assume 40" of usable fabric width for yardage.

Arrows indicate directions to press seams.

WOF – width of fabric
HST – half-square triangle ⧄
QST – quarter-square triangle ⊠

## CUTTING

### FROM WHITE PRINT CUT:

- 32 (2" x 3½") A rectangles
- 64 (2" x 3") C rectangles
- 32 (2" x 2½") E rectangles
- 7 (2½" x WOF) strips, stitch short ends to short ends, then subcut into:
  - 2 (2½" x 64½") O and 2 (2½" x 60½") N border strips

### FROM GREEN PRINT CUT:

- 16 (2" x 5½") D rectangles
- 16 (2" x 4½") B rectangles
- 16 (2" x 3½") A rectangles
- 16 (1½" x 2") F rectangles

### FROM RED PRINT CUT:

- 16 (2" x 8") H rectangles
- 16 (2" x 6½") G rectangles

### FROM BLUE PRINT CUT:

- 16 (2" x 9½") I rectangles
- 16 (2" x 8") H rectangles

### FROM RED CHECK CUT:

- 16 (2" x 11") J rectangles
- 16 (2" x 9½") I rectangles

### FROM BLUE SNOWFLAKE PRINT CUT:

- 16 (2" x 12½") K rectangles
- 16 (2" x 11") J rectangles

### FROM RED SNOWFLAKE PRINT CUT:

- 16 (2" x 14") L rectangles
- 16 (2" x 12½") K rectangles
- 8 (2½" x WOF) binding strips

### FROM BLUE CHECK CUT:

- 16 (2" x 15½") M rectangles
- 16 (2" x 14") L rectangles

### FROM GREEN CHECK CUT:

- 7 (3½" x WOF) strips, stitch short ends to short ends, then subcut into:
  2 (3½" x 70½") Q and 2 (3½" x 64½") P border strips

## COMPLETING THE BLOCKS

**1.** Mark a diagonal line on the wrong side of each white A and E rectangle and 32 of the white C rectangles in the orientations shown (Figure 1).

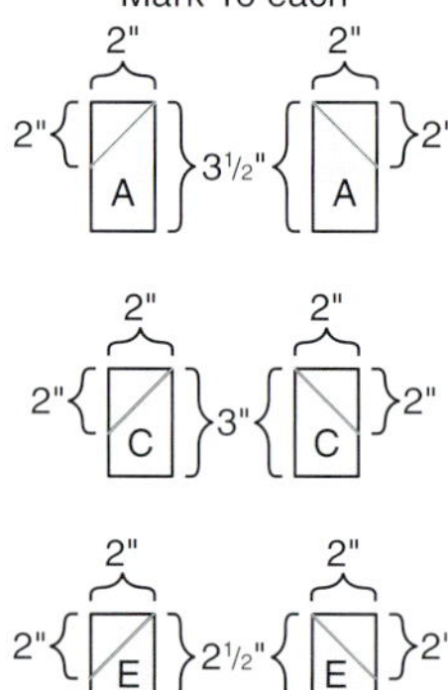


**Figure 1**

**2.** Refer to Sew & Flip Corners on page 7 and add two white A rectangles to each green A rectangle to make tree unit #1 (Figure 2). Make 16 tree unit #1 measuring 2" x 6½" from raw edge to raw edge.

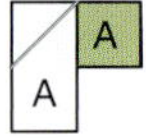

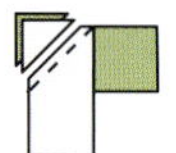
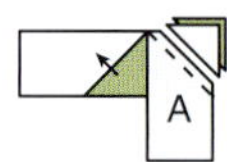

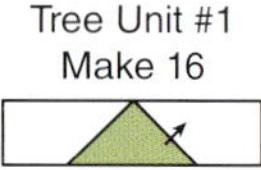


**Figure 2**

**3.** Using the same technique, make 16 each of tree unit #2 (Figure 3) and tree unit #3 (Figure 4).

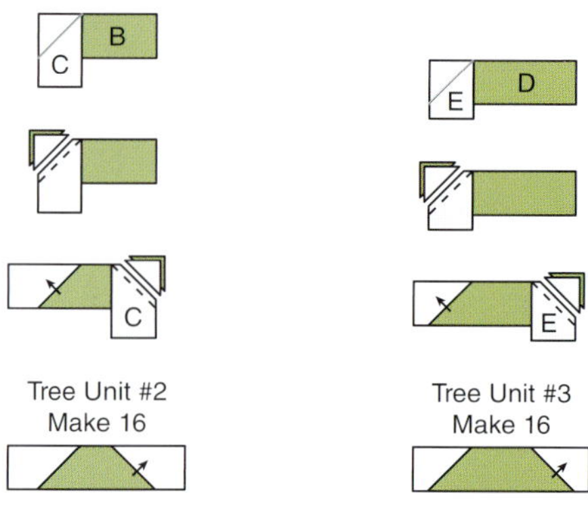


**Figure 3** **Figure 4**

**4.** Sew white C rectangles to the long sides of a green F rectangle to make tree unit #4 (Figure 5). Make 16 tree unit #4.

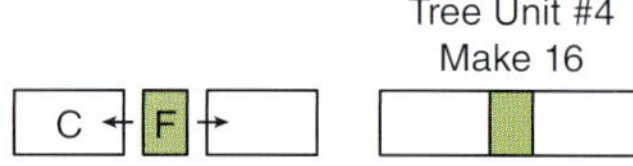


**Figure 5**

**5.** Sew together one each of tree units #1, #2, #3 and #4 to make a tree measuring 6½" x 6½" (Figure 6). Make 16.

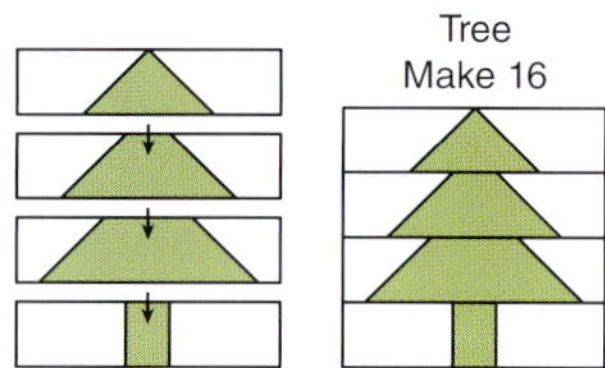


**Figure 6**

**6.** Arrange red print G and H rectangles, blue print H and I rectangles, red check I and J rectangles, blue snowflake print J and K rectangles, red snowflake print K and L rectangles and blue check L and M rectangles around a tree as shown (Figure 7). Sew the rectangles to the tree in counterclockwise alphabetical order beginning with the G rectangle to make a Log Cabin Tree block. Make 16.

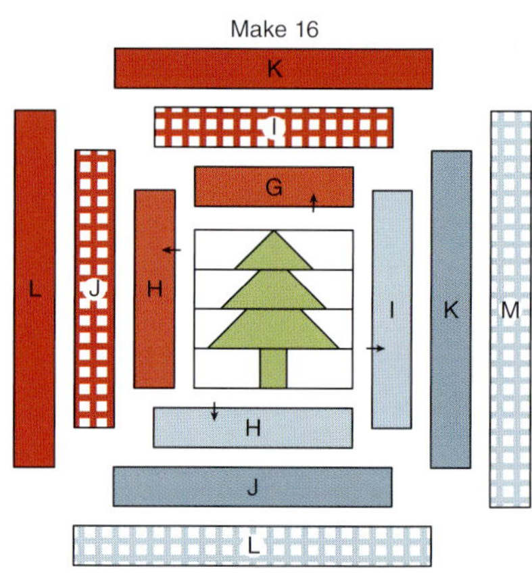


**Figure 7**

## Inspiration

*"For this quilt, I wanted to give traditional Log Cabin blocks a fun update with Christmas tree centers. The hardest part was choosing the block layout. There are lots of possibilities!" —Jen Daly*

## COMPLETING THE QUILT

**1.** Referring to the Assembly Diagram, lay out the blocks in four rows of four blocks each, noting the orientation of the blocks.

**2.** Sew the blocks into rows and join the rows to complete the quilt center. Press.

**3.** Sew the N–Q border strips to the quilt top in alphabetical order.

**4.** Layer, baste, quilt as desired and bind referring to Quilting Basics. The photographed quilt was quilted with the Christy's Jolly Holly pantograph by Christy Dillon from Urban Elementz. ■

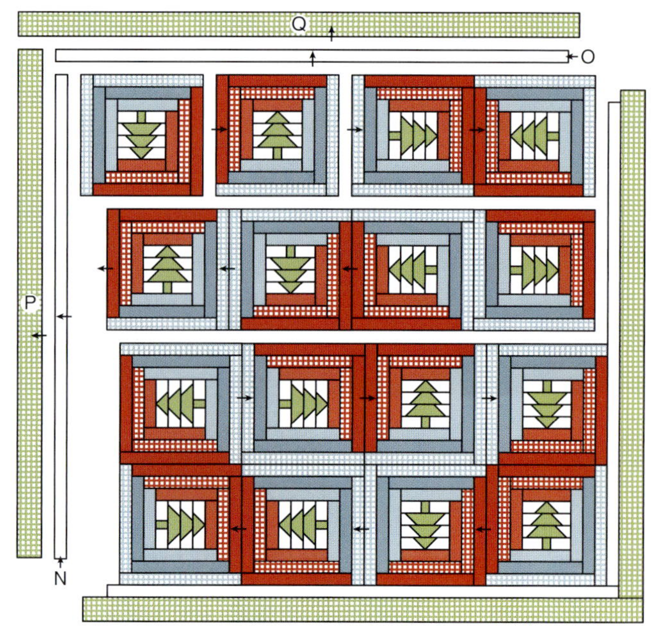


**Log Cabin Christmas**
Assembly Diagram 70" x 70"

# CHRISTMAS MOSAIC

Designed & Quilted by Jenny Kae Parks of Jenny Kae Quilts

Crafted with greens, reds and pinks against a sky of blues and purples, this unique Christmas tree can adorn any home for the holidays.

## MATERIALS

- ⅛ yard pale pink (P1)*
- ⅛ yard light pink (P2)*
- ⅛ yard medium pink (P3)*
- ⅛ yard hot pink (P4)*
- ⅛ yard dark berry pink (P5)*
- ⅛ yard pale yellow (Y1)*
- ⅛ yard bright yellow (Y2)*
- ⅛ yard light green (G1)*
- ⅛ yard chartreuse (G2)*
- ⅛ yard lime green (G3)*
- ¼ yard medium lime green (G4)*
- ¼ yard spruce green (G5)*
- ¼ yard dark teal green (G6)*
- ⅛ yard very dark teal green (G7)*
- ⅛ yard pale blue (B1)*
- ¼ yard aqua (B2)*
- ⅛ yard turquoise (B3)*
- ¼ yard light blue (B4)*
- ⅛ yard medium blue (B5)*
- ⅓ yard royal blue (B6)*
- ⅛ yard dark blue-green (B7)*
- ¼ yard indigo (B8)*
- ¼ yard cobalt (B9)*
- ⅛ yard periwinkle (R1)*
- ¼ yard purple (R2)*
- ¼ yard blue-violet (R3)*
- ⅛ yard dark purple (R4)*
- ¼ yard light brown (N1)*
- ⅛ yard dark brown (N2)*
- ⅛ yard white (W)*
- 1 yard black (K)*
- 3 yards backing*
- 47" x 59" batting
- Basic sewing tools and supplies

**Fabrics from Cherrywood Fabrics used to make sample.*

## SKILL LEVEL

Confident Beginner

## FINISHED SIZE

Quilt Size: 39" x 50"

## PROJECT NOTES

Read all instructions before beginning this project.

Stitch right sides together using a ¼" seam allowance unless otherwise specified.

Materials and cutting lists assume 40" of usable fabric width.

Arrows indicate directions to press seams.

WOF – width of fabric
HST – half-square triangle ⧄
QST – quarter-square triangle ☒

## CUTTING

### FROM PALE PINK (P1) CUT:

- 10 (2½") A squares
- 2 (1½") B squares

### FROM LIGHT PINK (P2) CUT:

- 4 (2½") A squares

### FROM MEDIUM PINK (P3) CUT:

- 5 (2½") A squares

### FROM HOT PINK (P4) CUT:

- 7 (2½") A squares

### FROM DARK BERRY PINK (P5) CUT:

- 8 (2½") A squares

### FROM PALE YELLOW (Y1) CUT:

- 4 (1½") B squares

## Inspiration

*"I found myself admiring a stack of green fabrics, ranging from soft, pale hues to deep evergreen tones. Nearby, another stack caught my eye, showcasing an array of blues and purples. As I studied them, I began to wonder: Could I arrange these fabrics to create the effect of a glowing Christmas tree set against a backdrop of a dark, starry night?" —Jenny Kae Parks*

### FROM BRIGHT YELLOW (Y2) CUT:

- 1 (2½") A square
- 1 C triangle

### FROM LIGHT GREEN (G1) CUT:

- 7 (2½") A squares

### FROM CHARTREUSE (G2) CUT:

- 10 (2½") A squares

### FROM LIME GREEN (G3) CUT:

- 9 (2½") A squares

### FROM MEDIUM LIME GREEN (G4) CUT:

- 20 (2½") A squares

### FROM SPRUCE GREEN (G5) CUT:

- 41 (2½") A squares

### FROM DARK TEAL GREEN (G6) CUT:

- 40 (2½") A squares

### FROM VERY DARK TEAL GREEN (G7) CUT:

- 10 (2½") A squares

### FROM PALE BLUE (B1) CUT:

- 10 (2½") A squares
- 2 (1½") B squares

### FROM AQUA (B2) CUT:

- 46 (2½") A squares

### FROM TURQUOISE (B3) CUT:

- 12 (2½") A squares

### FROM LIGHT BLUE (B4) CUT:

- 32 (2½") A squares

### FROM MEDIUM BLUE (B5) CUT:

- 8 (2½") A squares

### FROM ROYAL BLUE (B6) CUT:

- 40 (2½") A squares
- 8 C triangles

### FROM DARK BLUE-GREEN (B7) CUT:

- 12 (2½") A squares

### FROM INDIGO (B8) CUT:

- 19 (2½") A squares
- 7 C triangles

### FROM COBALT (B9) CUT:

- 9 (2½") A squares
- 7 C triangles
- 2 D triangles

### FROM PERIWINKLE (R1) CUT:

- 10 (2½") A squares

### FROM PURPLE (R2) CUT:

- 20 (2½") A squares

### FROM BLUE-VIOLET (R3) CUT:

- 7 (2½") A squares
- 6 C triangles
- 2 D triangles

### FROM DARK PURPLE (R4) CUT:

- 7 (2½") A squares
- 7 C triangles

### FROM LIGHT BROWN (N1) CUT:

- 14 (2½") A squares
- 12 C triangles
- 4 D triangles

### FROM DARK BROWN (N2) CUT:

- 4 (2½") A squares
- 3 C triangles

### FROM WHITE (W) CUT:

- 10 (2½") A squares

### FROM BLACK (K) CUT:

- 19 (2½") A squares
- 56 C triangles
- 6 (2½" x WOF) binding strips

## COMPLETING THE CENTER

**1.** Join together one pale pink (P1) square, two pale yellow (Y1) squares and one pale blue (B1) square to make one unit 1 (Figure 1). Repeat to make one unit 2.

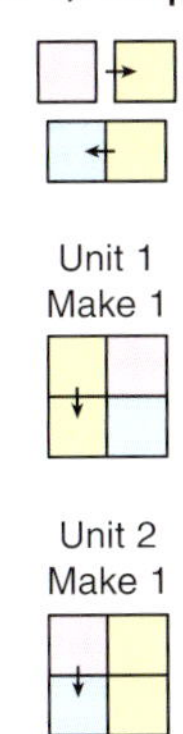


**Figure 1**

**2.** Arrange the A squares and units in the order shown in the Color Placement Diagram, paying close attention to the placement and orientation of the two units (Figure 2). Starting at the upper left corner, sew squares together in diagonal rows. Join rows together matching all seams. Press.

Figure 2

**3.** To trim, place a ruler along the edge. Align the ¼" line on the ruler where the three patches meet. Trim off the outer edges (Figure 3). Repeat on all sides to complete the quilt center. Sew a basting stitch ⅛" from the edge.

Figure 3

**4.** Join together two A squares, 23 C triangles and 2 D triangles in the colors shown to make top and bottom borders (Figure 4). Join together 31 C triangles and 2 D triangles in the colors shown to make left and right side borders.

Figure 4

## COMPLETING THE QUILT

**1.** Referring to the Assembly Diagram, sew the left and right borders to the sides of quilt center followed by the top and bottom borders.

**4.** Layer, baste, quilt as desired and bind referring to Quilting Basics. The photographed quilt was quilted with a wave design. ■

**Christmas Mosaic**
Assembly Diagram 39" x 50"

**Christmas Mosaic**
Color Placement Diagram

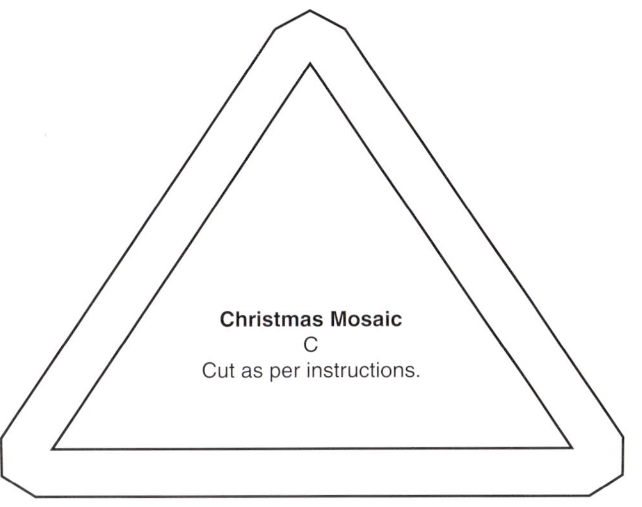


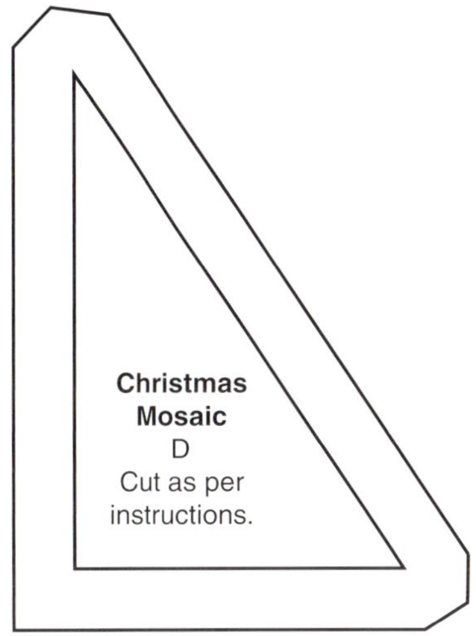

# SLEIGH RIDE

Designed & Quilted by Kim Ratchford of Stitched in Purple

Enjoy a sleigh ride through the snow-covered forest under the starlit sky.

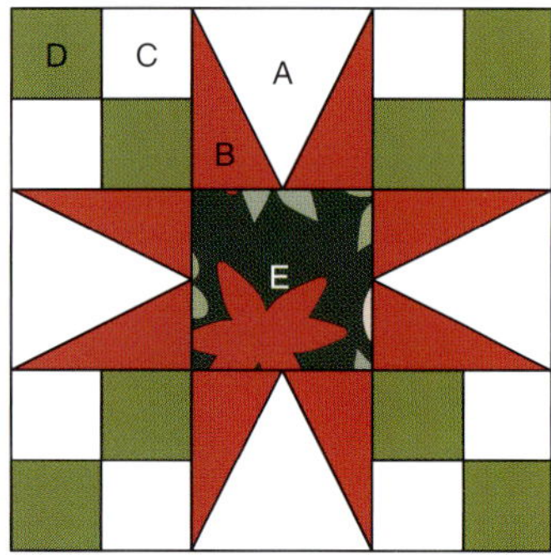


**Star**
12" x 12" Finished Block
Make 9

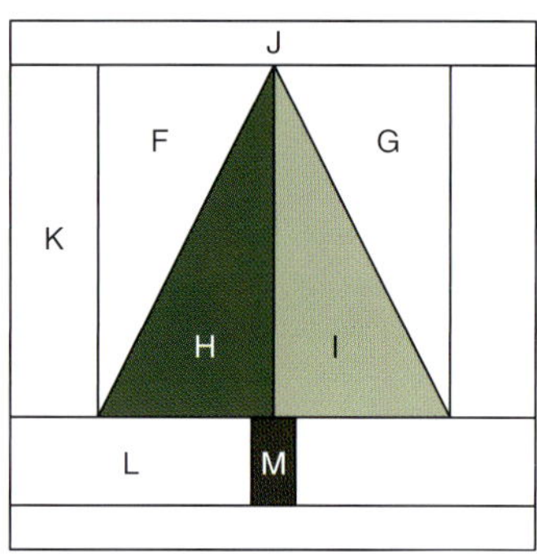


**Tree**
12" x 12" Finished Block
Make 12

**Chain**
12" x 12" Finished Block
Make 4

## SKILL LEVEL

Confident Beginner

## FINISHED SIZES

Quilt Size: 80½" x 80½"
Block Size: 12" x 12"
Number of Blocks: 25

## MATERIALS

- 5⅓ yards cream dot*
- 1⅛ yards red berry print*
- 1 yard medium green dot*
- 1½ yards dark green floral*
- ½ yard dark green berry print*
- ½ yard light green texture*
- 1 yard dark green texture*
- 7½ yards backing
- 89" x 89" batting*
- Basic sewing tools and supplies

**Fabrics from the Berry and Pine collection by Lella Boutique for Moda Fabrics; Dream 80/20 batting by Quilters Dream used to make sample. EQ8 was used to design this quilt.*

## PROJECT NOTES

Read all instructions before beginning this project.

Stitch right sides together using a ¼" seam allowance unless otherwise specified.

Materials and cutting lists assume 40" of usable fabric width.

Arrows indicate directions to press seams.

WOF – width of fabric
HST – half-square triangle ⧅
QST – quarter-square triangle ☒

HO
HO

## CUTTING

> **Here's a Tip**
>
> *Additional yardage may be needed if using directional prints for the half-rectangle triangle units.*

### FROM CREAM DOT CUT:

- 6 (5½" x 10") F rectangles
- 6 (5½" x 10") G rectangles
- 36 (5") A squares
- 16 (4½") N squares
- 40 (2½" x 12½") T rectangles
- 24 (2½" x 8½") K rectangles
- 24 (2½" x 6") L rectangles
- 16 (2½") O squares
- 7 (2½" x WOF) C strips
- 7 (2½" x WOF) strips, stitch short ends to short ends, then subcut into:
  2 (2½" x 68½") V and 2 (2½" x 72½") W border strips
- 2 (1½" x WOF) P strips
- 24 (1½" x 12½") J rectangles

### FROM RED BERRY PRINT CUT:

- 36 (4½" x 5½") B rectangles. With right sides up, cut once diagonally from top left corner to bottom right corner. ⧅
- 4 (4½") S squares
- 16 (2½") U squares

### FROM MEDIUM GREEN DOT CUT:

- 7 (2½" x WOF) D strips
- 1 (2½" x WOF) Q strip
- 2 (1½" x WOF) R strips

### FROM DARK GREEN FLORAL CUT:

- 9 (4½") E squares
- 8 (4½" x WOF) strips, stitch short ends to short ends, then subcut into:
  2 (4½" x 72½") X and 2 (4½" x 80½") Y border strips

### FROM DARK GREEN BERRY PRINT CUT:

- 6 (5½" x 10") H rectangles

### FROM LIGHT GREEN TEXTURE CUT:

- 6 (5½" x 10") I rectangles

### FROM DARK GREEN TEXTURE CUT:

- 9 (2½" x WOF) binding strips
- 12 (1½" x 2½") M rectangles

## COMPLETING THE STAR BLOCKS

**1.** Sew a C strip to a D strip along the long edges to make a C-D strip set (Figure 1). Make seven. Subcut into 88 (2½" x 4½") C-D units.

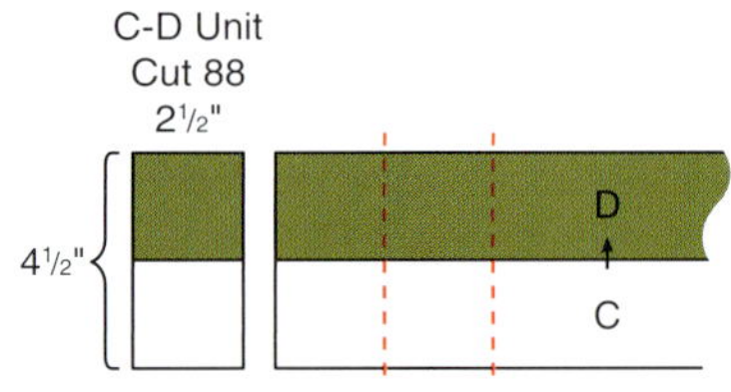


**Figure 1**

**2.** Join two C-D units together to make a four-patch unit (Figure 2). Make 36. The remaining 16 C-D units will be used later.

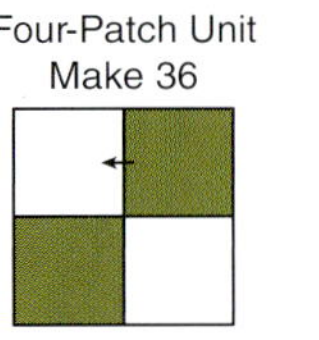


**Figure 2**

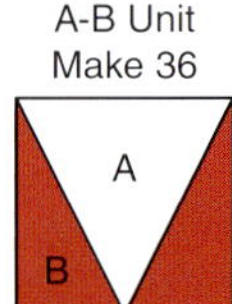


**Figure 3**

**3.** Make 36 copies of the foundation paper template at 100% scale/actual size. Refer to Paper Piecing on page 34 to make 36 A-B units (Figure 3).

**4.** Lay out four four-patch units, four A-B units and one E square in three rows. Join rows to complete a Star block (Figure 4). Make nine.

**Figure 4**

## COMPLETING THE TREE BLOCKS

**1.** With all rectangles facing right sides up, cut six F rectangles diagonally from the bottom left corner to the top right corner, creating 12 F triangles (Figure 5).

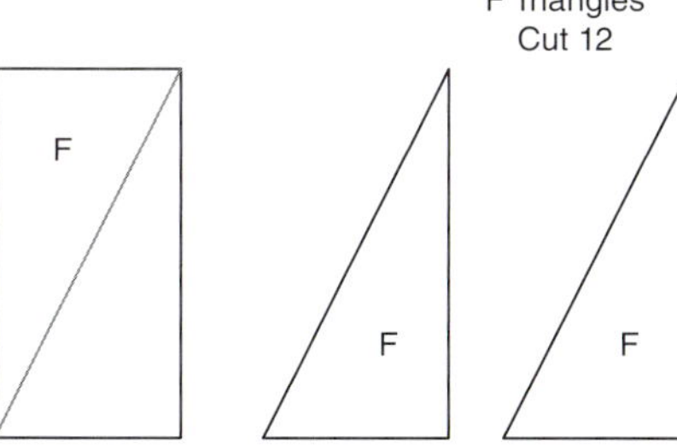


**Figure 5**

**2.** With all rectangles facing right sides up, cut six G rectangles diagonally from the bottom right corner to the top left corner, creating 12 G triangles (Figure 6).

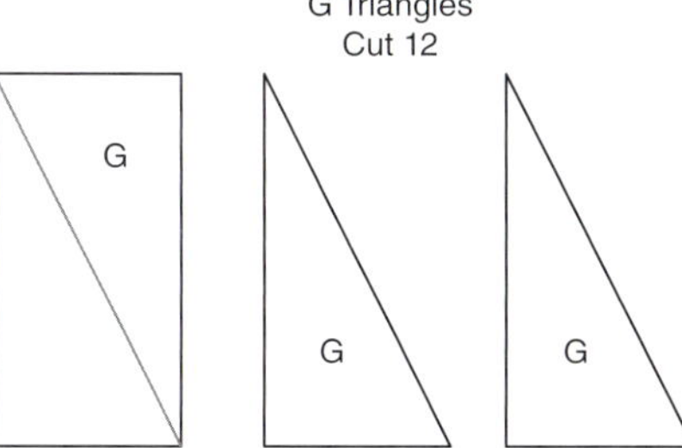


**Figure 6**

**3.** With all rectangles facing right sides up, cut six H rectangles diagonally from the bottom left corner to the top right corner, creating 12 H triangles (Figure 7).

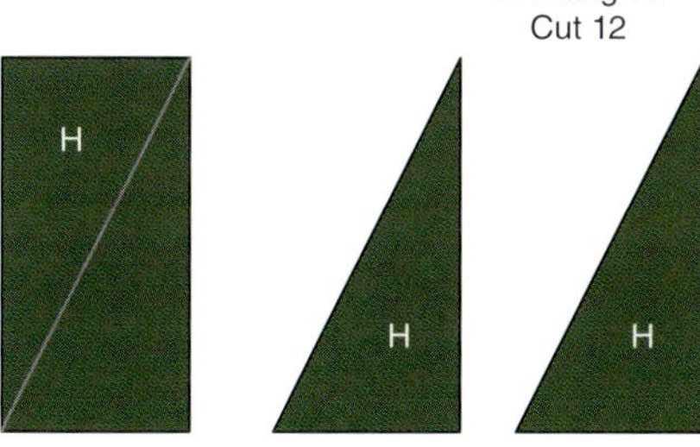


**Figure 7**

**4.** With all rectangles facing right sides up, cut six I rectangles diagonally from the bottom right corner to the top left corner, creating 12 I triangles (Figure 8).

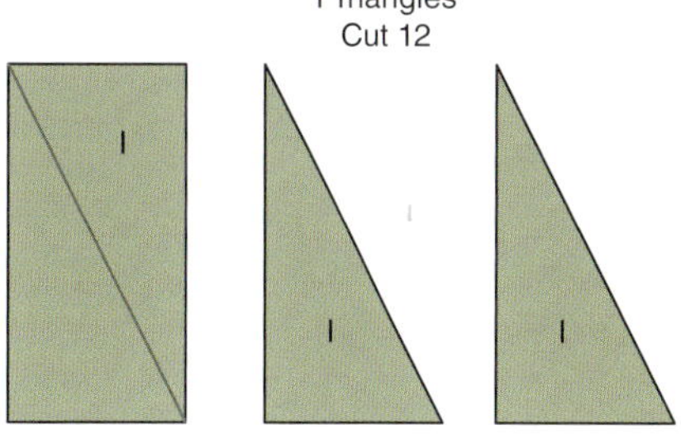


**Figure 8**

**5.** Sew an F triangle to an H triangle along the diagonal sides, overlapping edges ¼", to complete an F-H unit (Figure 9). Make 12. Trim to 4½" x 8½". To trim, align your ruler with the diagonal seam of the triangle, ensuring the ¼" marks on the ruler fall directly on the seam line, then trim the top and right edges of the triangle, rotating it 180 degrees to trim the other side.

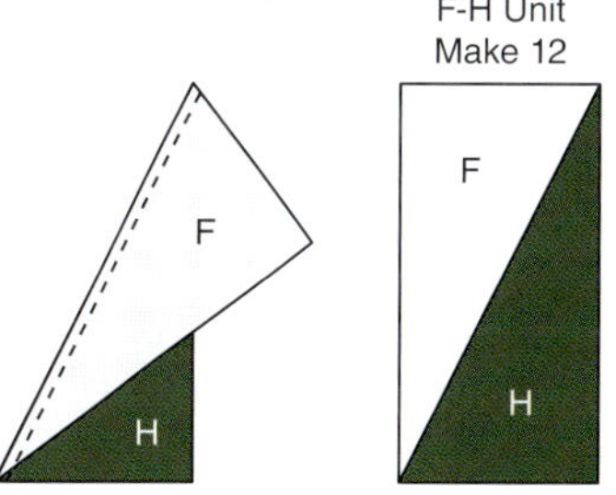


**Figure 9**

**6.** Sew an I triangle to a G triangle along the diagonal sides, overlapping edges ¼", to complete an I-G unit (Figure 10). Make 12. Trim to 4½" x 8½".

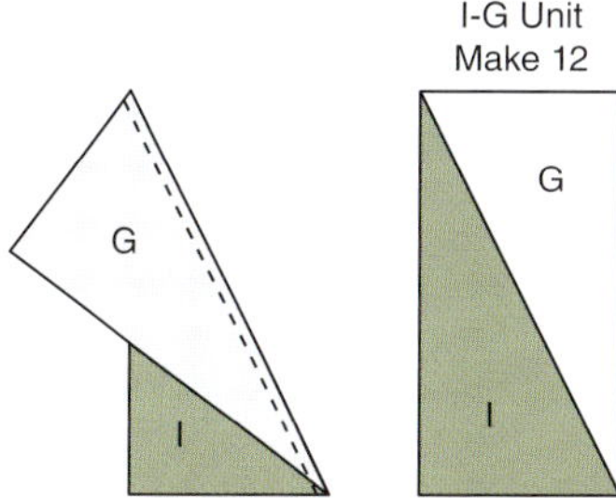


**Figure 10**

**7.** Lay out an F-H unit, an I-G unit, two K rectangles, two L rectangles and one M rectangle into two rows; join together. Join rows and sew J rectangles to top and bottom to complete a Tree block (Figure 11). Make 12.

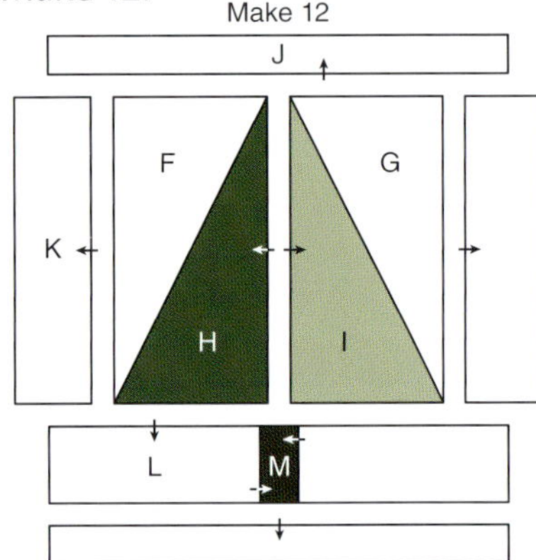


**Figure 11**

## COMPLETING THE CHAIN BLOCKS

**1.** Sew a P strip to an R strip along the long edges (Figure 12). Subcut into 32 (1½" x 2½") P-R units. Join two P-R units together to make a four-patch unit. Make 16.

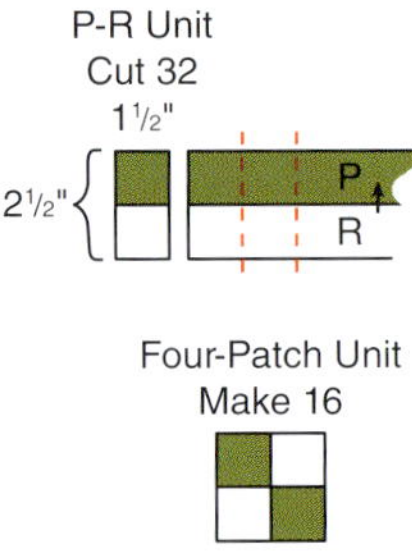


**Figure 12**

**2.** Paying close attention to the orientation of the four-patch unit, sew an O square to the top of a four-patch unit (Figure 13). Sew a C-D unit to the left side to complete a corner unit. Make 16.

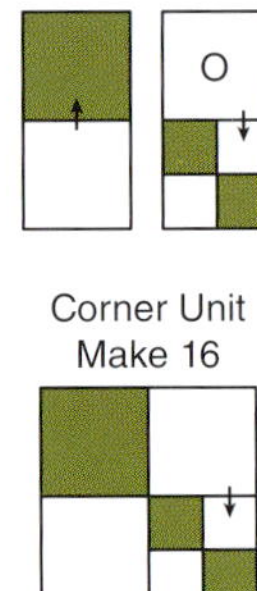


**Figure 13**

**3.** Lay out four corner units, four N squares and one S square in three rows. Join rows to complete a Chain block (Figure 14). Make four.

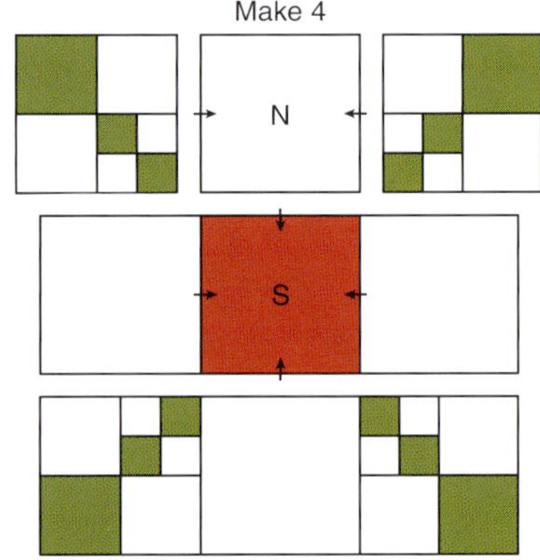


**Figure 14**

## COMPLETING THE QUILT

**1.** Referring to the Assembly Diagram, lay out the blocks, T rectangles and U squares in nine rows, noting the placement of the blocks.

**2.** Sew the blocks and patches into rows and join the rows to complete the quilt center. Press.

**3.** Sew the V–Y border strips to the quilt top in alphabetical order.

**4.** Layer, baste, quilt as desired and bind referring to Quilting Basics. The photographed quilt was quilted with an overall swirl design. ■

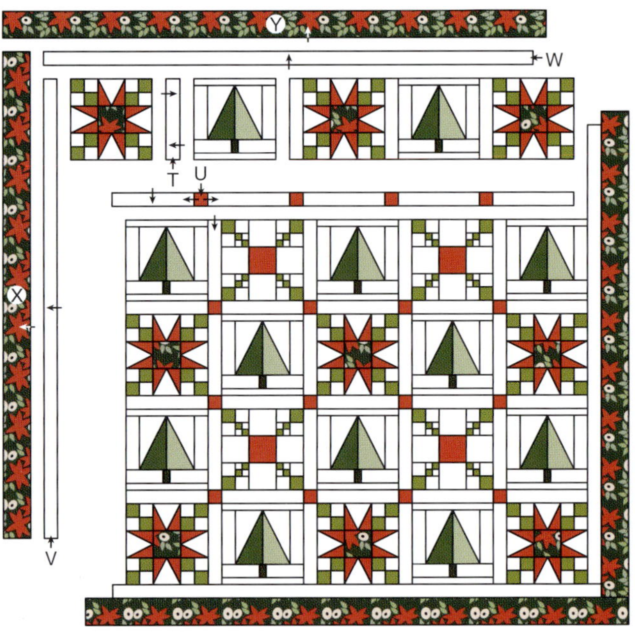


**Sleigh Ride**
Assembly Diagram 80½" x 80½"

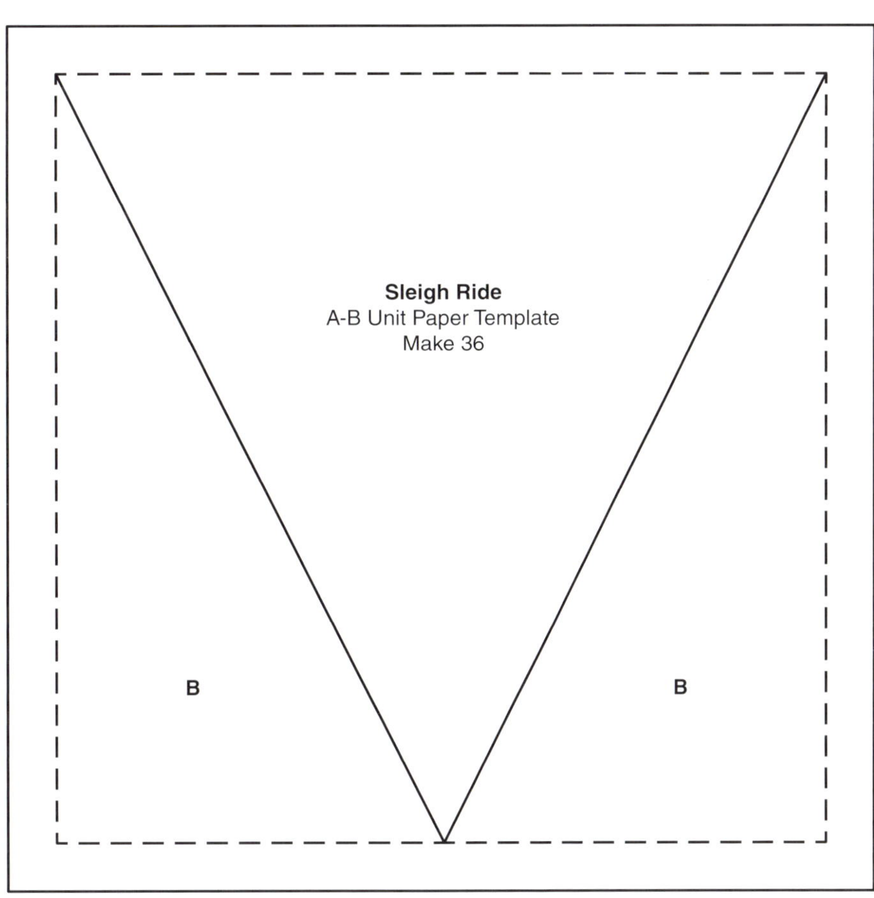
Sleigh Ride
A-B Unit Paper Template
Make 36
B
B

# PAPER PIECING

Paper piecing allows a quilter to make blocks with odd-shaped and/or small pieces and more precise corners. Fabric pieces are sewn together onto the reverse side of a paper-piecing pattern, and then the paper is carefully removed when the block is completed. You may have to rethink how you piece when using this technique, and it does require a little more yardage.

**1.** Make same-size copies of the paper-piecing pattern as directed in the pattern. There are several choices in transparent papers as well as water-soluble papers that can be used, which are available at your local office supply store, quilt shop or online. Some papers can be used in your printer.

**2.** Cut out the patterns, leaving a margin around the outside bold lines as shown in Figure A. All patterns are reversed on the paper copies. Pattern color choices can be written in each numbered space on the marked side of each copy.

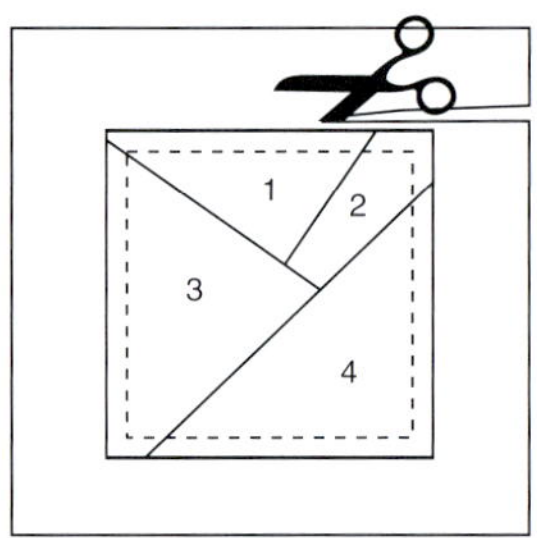


Figure A

**3.** When cutting fabric for paper piecing, the pieces do not have to be the exact size and shape of the area to be covered. Cut fabric pieces the general shape and ¼"–½" larger than the design area to be covered. This makes paper piecing a good way to use up scraps.

**4.** With the printed side of the pattern facing you, fold along each line of the pattern as shown in Figure B, creasing the stitching lines. This will help in trimming the fabric seam allowances and in removing the paper when you are finished stitching. ***Note:*** *You can also machine-stitch along the lines with a basting stitch and no thread to perforate the paper.*

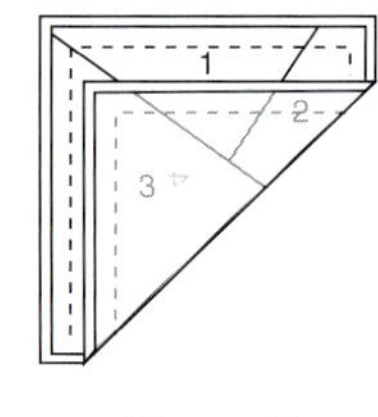


Figure B

**5.** Turn the paper pattern over with the unmarked side facing you and position fabric indicated on pattern right side up over the space marked 1. Hold the paper up to a window or over a light box to make sure that the fabric overlaps all sides of space 1 at least ¼" as shown in Figure C from the printed side of the pattern. Pin to hold fabric in place. ***Note:*** *You can also use a light touch of glue stick. Too much glue will make the paper difficult to remove.*

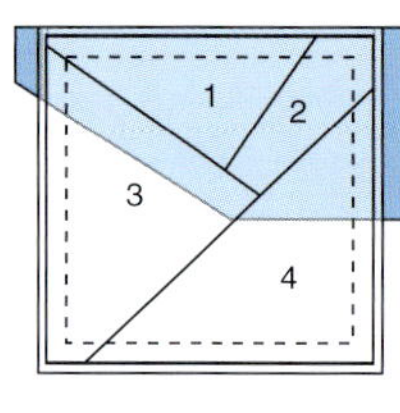


Figure C

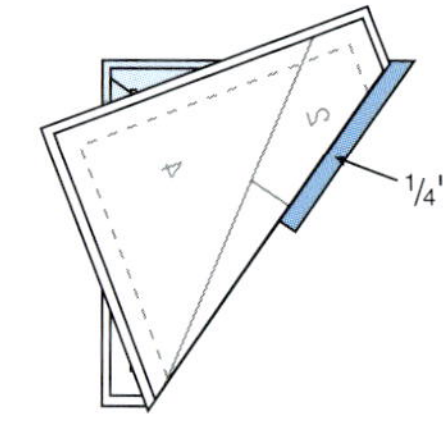


Figure D

**6.** Turn the paper over with the right side of the paper facing you, and fold the paper along the lines between sections 1 and 2. Trim fabric to about ¼" from the folded edge as shown in Figure D.

**7.** Place the second fabric indicated right sides together with first piece. Fabric edges should be even along line between spaces 1 and 2 as shown in Figure E. Fold fabric over and check to see if second fabric piece will cover space 2.

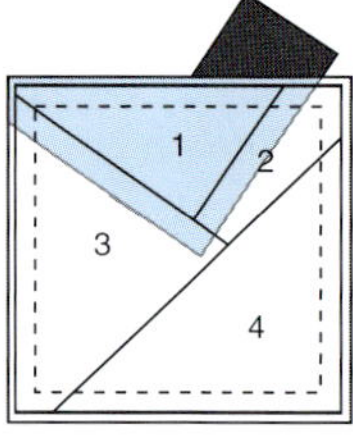


Figure E

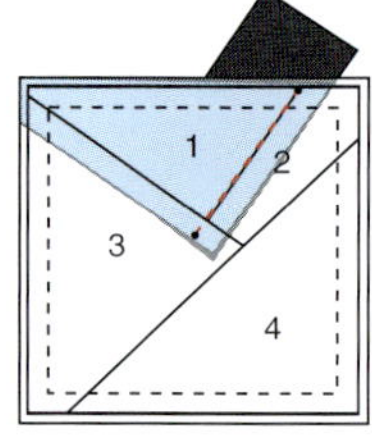


Figure F

**8.** With the right side of the paper facing you, hold fabric pieces together and stitch along the line between spaces 1 and 2 as shown in Figure F using a very small stitch length (18–20 stitches per inch). ***Note:*** *Using a smaller stitch length will make removing paper easier because it creates a tear line at the seam. Always begin and end seam by sewing two to three stitches beyond the line. You do not need to backstitch. Start sewing at the solid outside line of the pattern when the beginning of the seam is at the edge of the pattern.*

**9.** Turn the pattern over, flip the second fabric back and finger-press as shown in Figure G.

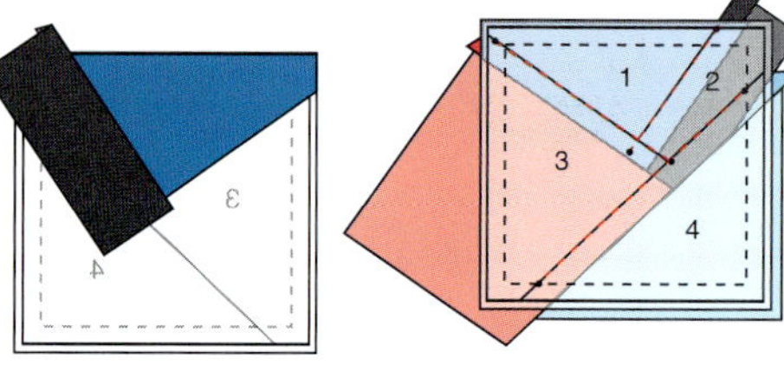


Figure G Figure H

**10.** Continue trimming and sewing pieces in numerical order until the pattern is completely covered. Make sure pieces along the outer edge extend past the solid line to allow for a ¼" seam allowance as shown in Figure H.

**11.** When the whole block is sewn, press the block and trim all excess fabric from the block along the outside-edge solid line of the paper pattern as shown in Figure I.

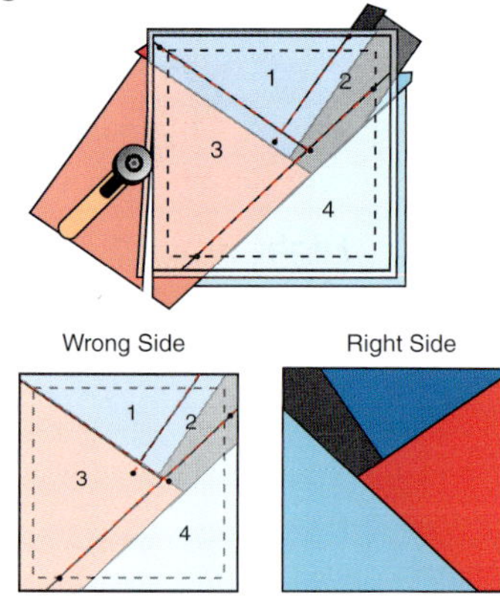


Figure I

**12.** After stitching blocks together, carefully remove the backing paper from completed blocks and press seams. You can also staystitch ⅛" from the outer edge of the completed block. Carefully remove backing paper and press seams. Then complete quilt top assembly.

# FESTIVE YULETIDE

Designed & Quilted by Joy Heimark

Celebrate the warmth and cheer of the holiday season under this timeless quilt. Whether draped over your sofa or spread across the bed, this quilt will bring the magic of Christmas into your home.

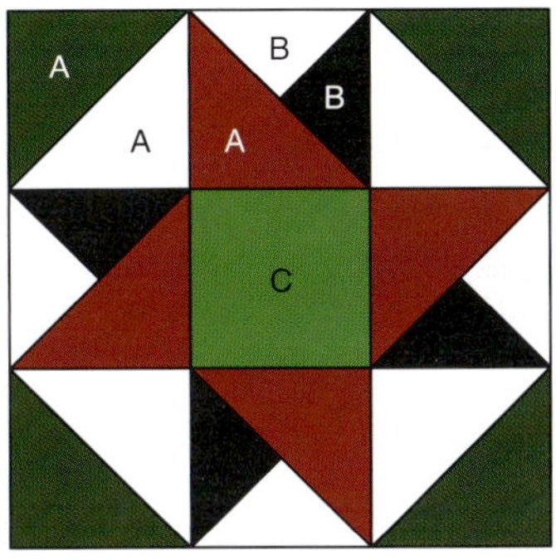


**Left Block 1**
9" x 9" Finished Block
Make 2

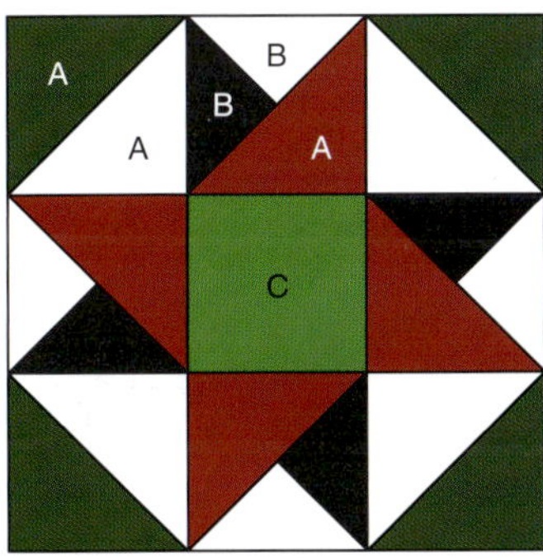


**Right Block 1**
9" x 9" Finished Block
Make 2

## SKILL LEVEL

Intermediate

## FINISHED SIZES

Quilt Size: 66" x 66"
Block Size: 9" x 9"
Number of Blocks: 24

## MATERIALS

- ⅞ yard dark green solid
- 1⅛ yards white solid
- 1¾ yards black solid
- ⅞ yard light green solid
- 1¾ yards red solid
- 1¾ yards black print
- 4½ yards backing
- 74" x 74" batting
- Basic sewing tools and supplies

## PROJECT NOTES

Read all instructions before beginning this project.

Stitch right sides together using a ¼" seam allowance unless otherwise specified.

Materials and cutting lists assume 40" of usable fabric width.

Arrows indicate directions to press seams.

WOF – width of fabric
HST – half-square triangle
QST – quarter-square triangle

## CUTTING

### FROM DARK GREEN SOLID CUT:

- 16 (4½") D squares
- 22 (4") A squares
- 8 (3½") H squares

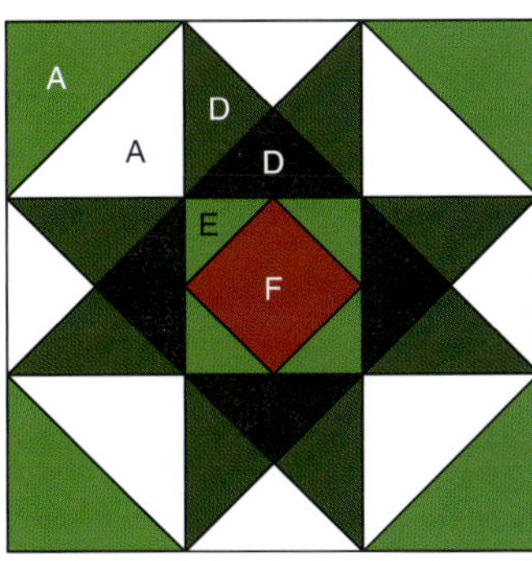


**Block #2**
9" x 9" Finished Block
Make 8

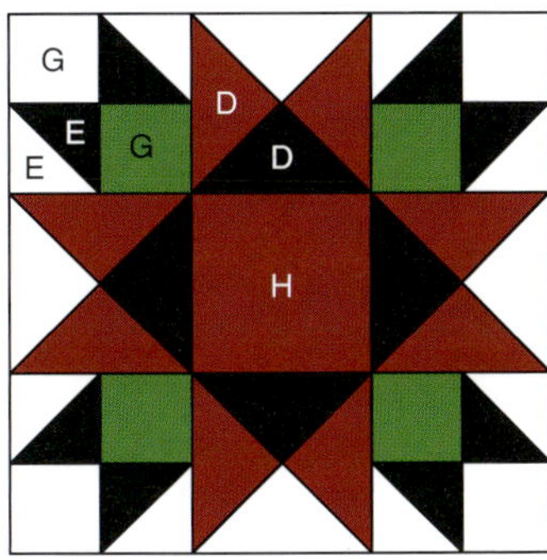


**Block #3**
9" x 9" Finished Block
Make 4

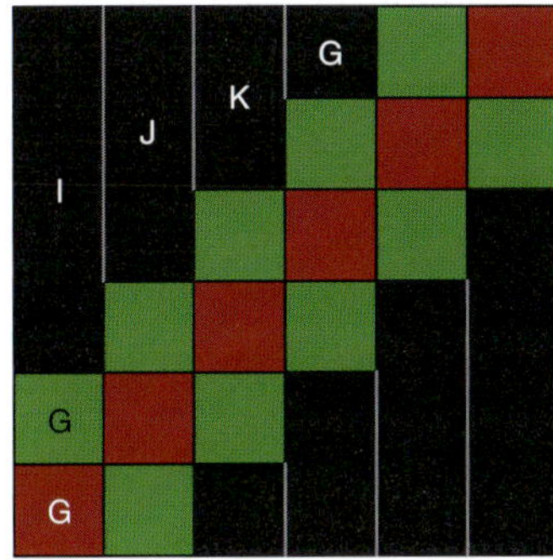


**Block #4**
9" x 9" Finished Block
Make 8

## FROM WHITE SOLID CUT:

- 12 (4½") D squares
- 4 (4¼") B squares
- 40 (4") A squares
- 16 (2½") E squares
- 16 (2") G squares

## FROM BLACK SOLID CUT:

- 12 (4½") D squares
- 4 (4¼") B squares
- 16 (2½" x 6½") I rectangles
- 16 (2½" x 5") J rectangles
- 16 (2½" x 3½") K rectangles
- 16 (2½") E squares
- 16 (2") G squares
- 7 (2" x WOF) strips, stitch short ends to short ends, then subcut into the following border strips:
  2 (2" x 24½") L
  2 (2" x 27½") M
  2 (2" x 33½") N
  2 (2" x 36½") O

## Inspiration

*"I like medallion quilts, so I enjoyed creating this pattern which is a mix of many different borders surrounding a center square of four blocks."* —*Joy Heimark*

### FROM LIGHT GREEN SOLID CUT:

- 16 (4") A squares
- 4 (3½") C squares
- 16 (2½") E squares
- 96 (2") G squares

### FROM RED SOLID CUT:

- 8 (4½") D squares
- 38 (4") A squares
- 4 (3½") H squares
- 8 (2⅝") F squares
- 6 (2" x WOF) strips, stitch short ends to short ends, then subcut into:
  7 (2" x 54½") P and 2 (2" x 57½") Q border strips
- 48 (2") G squares

### FROM BLACK PRINT CUT:

- 7 (5" x WOF) strips, stitch short ends to short ends, then subcut into:
  2 (5" x 57½") R and 2 (5" x 66½") S border strips
- 7 (2½" x WOF) binding strips

## COMPLETING THE BLOCKS

**1.** Refer to Half-Square Triangles and use dark green and white A squares to make 16 A-A units (Figure 1). Trim to 3½" x 3½".

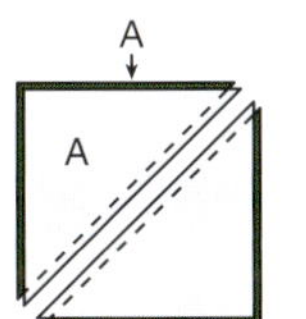

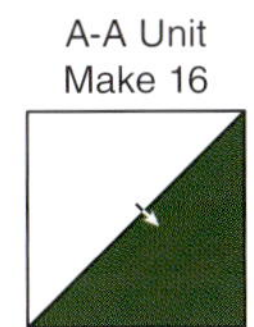


**Figure 1**

**2.** In the same way, use white and black B squares to make eight B-B units (Figure 2).

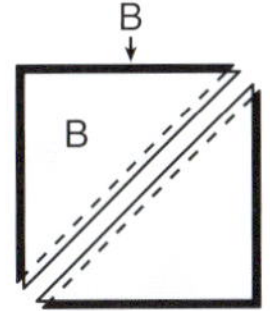

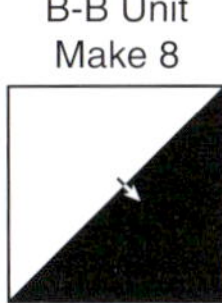


**Figure 2**

**3.** Draw a diagonal line on the wrong side of each B-B unit. Place a B-B unit on top of a red A square, right sides together, and stitch a scant ¼" on each side of the drawn line. Cut on drawn line to make one A-B-B left unit and one A-B-B right unit (Figure 3). Trim to 3½" x 3½". Make eight of each.

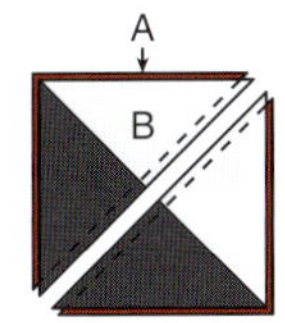

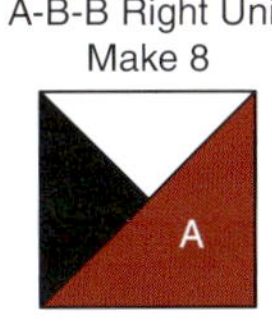

**Figure 3**

**4.** Join four A-A units, four A-B-B left units and one light green C square into three rows. Join rows to complete a Left Block 1 (Figure 4). Trim to 9½" x 9½". Make two.

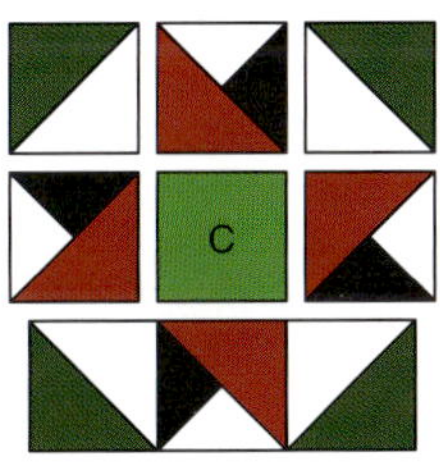

**Figure 4**

## HALF-SQUARE TRIANGLES

Half-square triangles (HSTs) are a basic unit of quilting used in many blocks or on their own. This construction method will yield two HSTs.

**1.** Refer to the pattern for size to cut squares. The standard formula is to add ⅞" to the finished size of the square. Cut two squares from different colors this size. For example, for a 3" finished HST unit, cut 3⅞" squares.

**2.** Draw a diagonal line from corner to corner on the wrong side of the lightest color square. Layer the squares right sides together. Stitch ¼" on either side of the drawn line (Figure A).

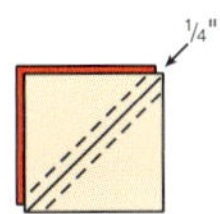


**Figure A**

**3.** Cut the squares apart on the drawn line, leaving a ¼" seam allowance and making two HST units referring to Figure B.

**Figure B**

**4.** Open the HST units and press seam allowances toward the darker fabric making two HST units (Figure C). ●

**Figure C**

**5.** Join four A-A units, four A-B-B right units and one light green C square into three rows. Join rows to complete a Right Block 1 (Figure 5). Trim to 9½" x 9½". Make two.

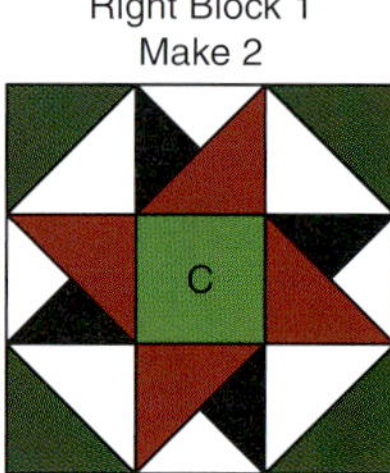


**Figure 5**

**6.** Refer to Quarter-Square Triangles and use dark green, white and black D squares to make 32 dark green QST units (Figure 6). Trim to 3½" x 3½".

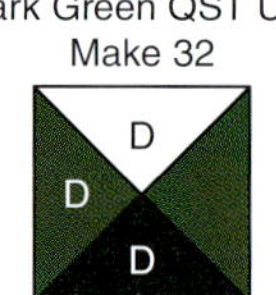


**Figure 6**

**7.** Cut eight light green E squares in half diagonally. Sew two triangles to opposite sides of a red F square. Sew two triangles to the remaining sides to make an E-F unit (Figure 7). Trim to 3½" x 3½". Make eight.

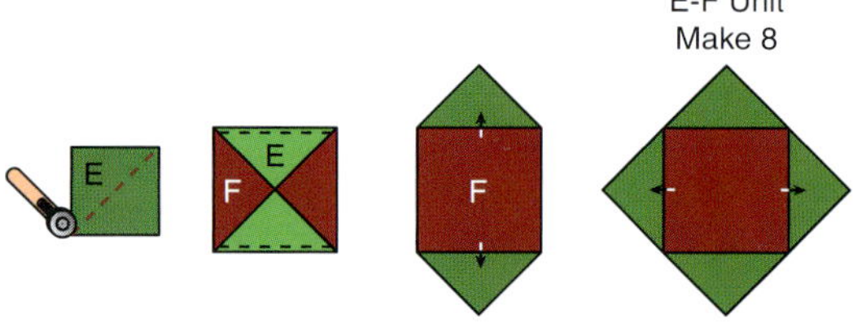


**Figure 7**

**8.** Refer again to Half-Square Triangles and use light green and white A squares to make 32 light green A-A units (Figure 8). Trim to 3½" x 3½".

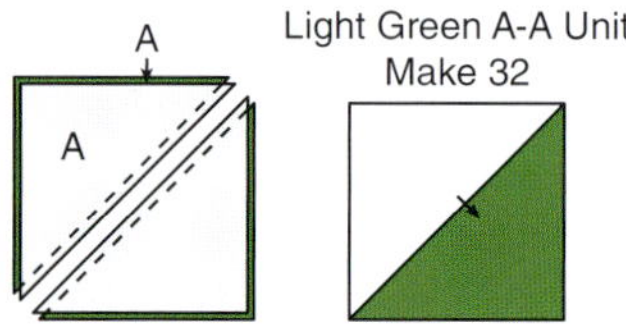


**Figure 8**

**9.** Lay out four QST units, four light green A-A units and one E-F unit (Figure 9). Sew into rows. Sew rows together to complete a Block 2. Trim to 9½" x 9½". Make eight.

**Figure 9**

**10.** Refer again to Half-Square Triangles and use black and white E squares to make 32 black E-E units (Figure 10). Trim to 2" x 2".

**Figure 10**

**11.** Refer again to Quarter-Square Triangles and use red, white and black D squares to make 16 red QST units (Figure 11). Trim to 3½" x 3½".

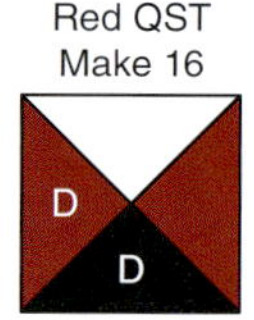


**Figure 11**

**12.** Lay out one white G square, one light green G square and two black E-E units (Figure 12). Sew into rows. Sew rows together to complete a four-patch unit. Make 16.

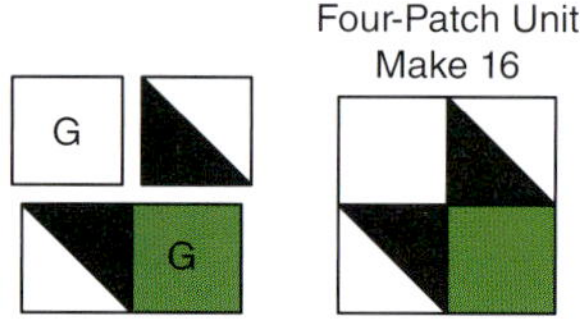


**Figure 12**

**13.** Lay out four four-patch units, four red QST units and one red H square (Figure 13). Sew into rows. Sew rows together to complete a Block 3. Trim to 9½" x 9½". Make four.

Block 3
Make 4

**Figure 13**

**14.** Lay out six red G squares, 10 light green G squares, two black G squares, two black K rectangles, two black J rectangles and two black I rectangles (Figure 14). Sew into vertical rows. Sew rows together to complete a Block 4. Trim to 9½" x 9½". Make eight.

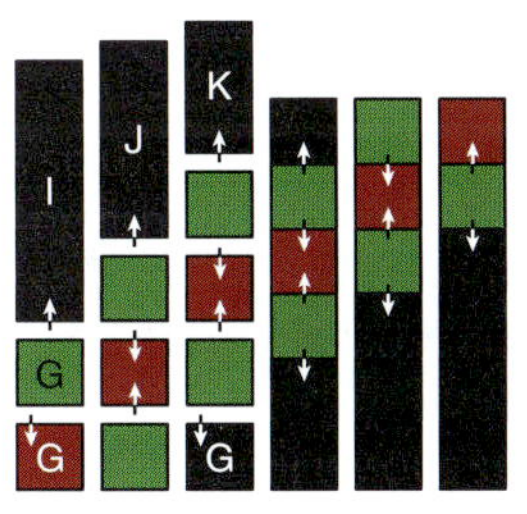


Block 4
Make 8

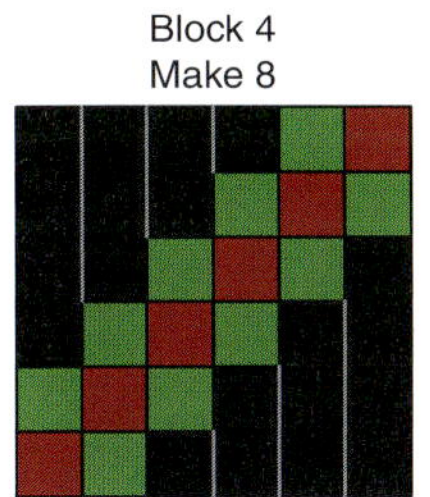

**Figure 14**

## QUARTER-SQUARE TRIANGLES

Quarter-square triangles (QSTs) are a basic unit of quilting used in many blocks or on their own. This construction method will yield two QST units.

**1.** Refer to the pattern for size to cut squares. The standard formula is to add 1¼" to the finished size of the square. Cut two squares from different colors this size. For example, for a 3" finished QST unit, cut 4¼" squares.

**2.** Draw a diagonal line from corner to corner on the wrong side of the lightest color square. Layer the squares right sides together. Stitch ¼" on either side of the drawn line. Cut apart on the drawn line to yield two half-square triangle (HST) units. Open and press toward the darker fabric (Figure A).

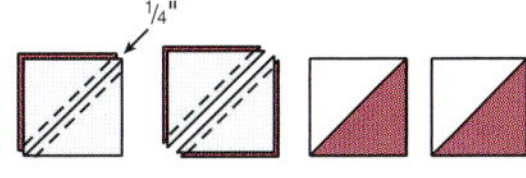


**Figure A**

**3.** Draw a diagonal line from corner to corner on the wrong side of one HST unit perpendicular to the seam line (Figure B). Place the two HST units right sides together with opposite colors facing one another. Stitch ¼" on either side of the drawn line.

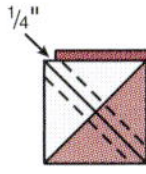


**Figure B**

**4.** Cut apart on the drawn line, leaving a ¼" seam allowance and making two QST units (Figure C).

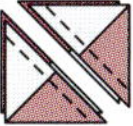

**Figure C**

**5.** Open and press to complete two QST units, also known as hourglass units when made of two contrasting fabrics (Figure D). ●

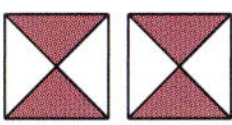

**Figure D**

## COMPLETING THE QUILT

**1.** Refer to the Assembly Diagram for the following steps. Lay out the four block 1s, noting the orientation of the blocks. Sew into rows. Sew rows together to complete the quilt center.

**2.** Refer again to Half-Square Triangles and use red and dark green A squares to make 28 red/dark green A-A units (Figure 15). Trim to 3½" x 3½".

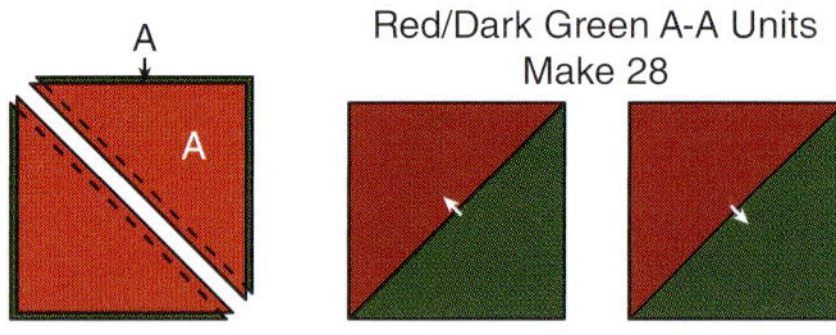


**Figure 15**

**3.** Join six red/dark green A-A units together. Make two and join to sides of quilt center.

**4.** Join eight red/dark green A-A units together. Make two and join to top and bottom of quilt center.

**5.** Sew the black L and M border strips to the quilt top in alphabetical order.

**6.** Refer again to Half-Square Triangles and use red and white A squares to make 32 red/white A-A units (Figure 16). Trim to 3½" x 3½".

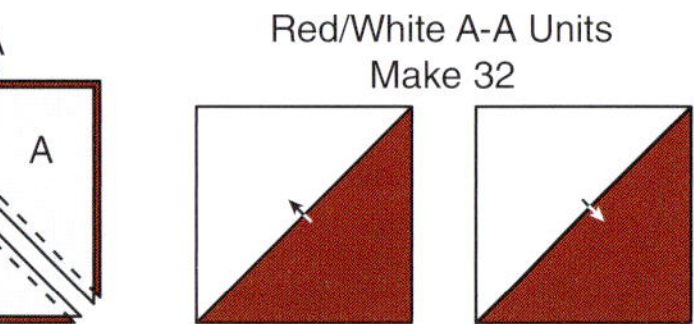


**Figure 16**

**7.** Join eight red/white A-A units and one dark green H square together. Make two and join to sides of quilt center.

**8.** Join eight red/white A-A units and three dark green H squares together. Make two and join to top and bottom of quilt center.

**9.** Sew the N and O border strips to the quilt top in alphabetical order.

**10.** Lay out two Block 4s and two Block 2s, and sew into a row. Make two and sew to sides of quilt.

**11.** Lay out two Block 4s, two Block 2s and two Block 3s, and sew into a row. Make two and sew to top and bottom of quilt.

**12.** Sew the P and Q border strips to the quilt top in alphabetical order.

**13.** Sew the R and S border strips to the quilt top in alphabetical order.

**14.** Layer, baste, quilt as desired and bind referring to Quilting Basics. The photographed quilt was quilted with a meander design. ■

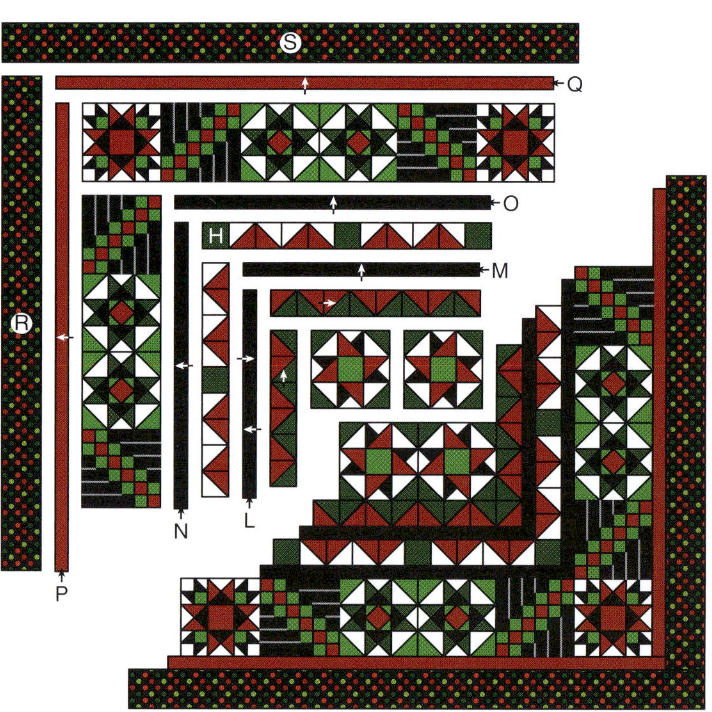


**Festive Yuletide**
Assembly Diagram 66" x 66"

# COZY LOG CABIN RUNNER

Designed & Quilted by Debra Clutter

Gather your favorite 10" squares or Christmas fabrics to create this quick and easy table runner.

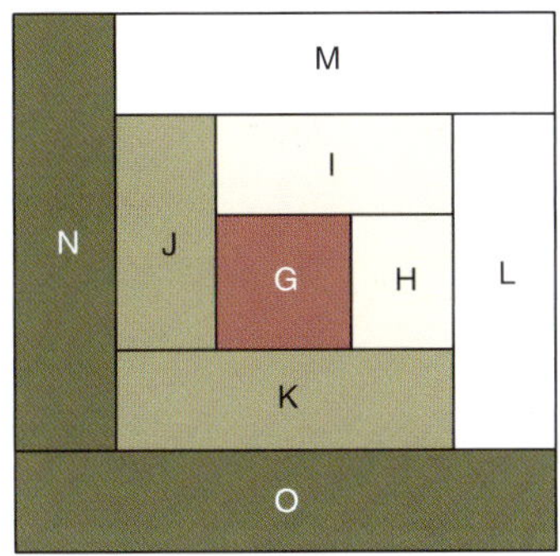


**Log Cabin**
8" x 8" Finished Block
Make 2

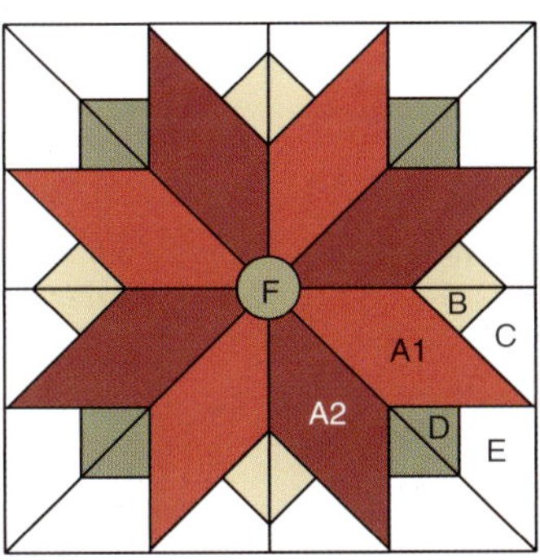


**Poinsettia**
8" x 8" Finished Block
Make 1

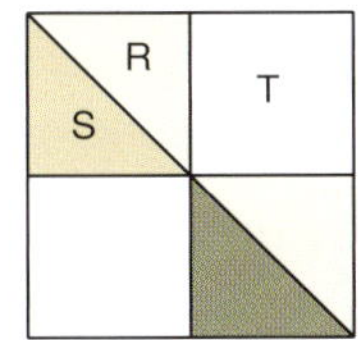


**Four-Patch**
4" x 4" Finished Block
Make 20

## SKILL LEVEL

Intermediate

## FINISHED SIZES

Runner Size: 18" x 34"
Block Size: 4" x 4" and 8" x 8"
Number of Blocks: 20 and 3

## MATERIALS

- ½ yard white
- 1 fat quarter cream snowflake print
- 1 fat quarter red solid
- 9 (10") squares (1 dark green, 2 greens, 2 reds, 1 tan and 3 additional dark prints)
- 1 yard backing fabric
- 22" x 38" batting
- Paper for foundation piecing
- Scrap of paper-backed fusible web
- Thread
- Basic sewing tools and supplies

## PROJECT NOTES

Read all instructions before beginning this project.

Stitch right sides together using a ¼" seam allowance unless otherwise specified.

Materials and cutting lists assume 40" of usable fabric width for yardage and 20" for fat quarters.

Arrows indicate directions to press seams.

WOF – width of fabric
HST – half-square triangle ⧅
QST – quarter-square triangle ⊠

## CUTTING

### FROM WHITE CUT:

- 44 (2½") T squares
- 8 (2" x 2¼") C rectangles
- 2 (2" x 7") M strips
- 2 (2" x 5½") L strips
- 8 (1¾" x 3½") E rectangles

### FROM CREAM SNOWFLAKE PRINT CUT:

- 6 (5¾") R squares
- 2 (2" x 4") I strips
- 2 (2" x 2½") H strips

### FROM RED SOLID CUT:

- 1 (5¾") S square
- 4 (2¾" x 4½") A rectangles
- 4 (1½" x WOF) P/Q strips, stitch short ends to short ends, then subcut into:
  2 (1½" x 24½") P and
  2 (1½" x 10½") Q border strips

### FROM DARK GREEN 10" SQUARE CUT:

- 2 (2" x 8½") O strips
- 2 (2" x 7") N strips

### FROM GREEN #1 10" SQUARE CUT:

- 2 (2" x 5½") K strips
- 2 (2" x 4") J strips

### FROM GREEN #2 10" SQUARE CUT:

- 8 (1¾" x 3½") D rectangles

### FROM RED #1 10" SQUARE CUT:

- 4 (2¾" x 4½") A rectangles

### FROM RED #2 10" SQUARE CUT:

- 1 (5¾") S square
- 2 (2½") G squares

### FROM TAN 10" SQUARE CUT:

- 1 (5¾") S square
- 8 (1¾") B squares

### FROM 3 ADDITIONAL DARK 10" SQUARES CUT:

- 1 (5¾") S square (3 total)

## COMPLETING THE BLOCKS

### POINSETTIA BLOCK

**1.** Prepare four copies of each of the paper piecing foundations provided on page 45.

**2.** Refer to Paper Piecing on page 34 and paper-piece four of each A, B, C and D foundation (Figure 1). Trim foundation units along outside solid line.

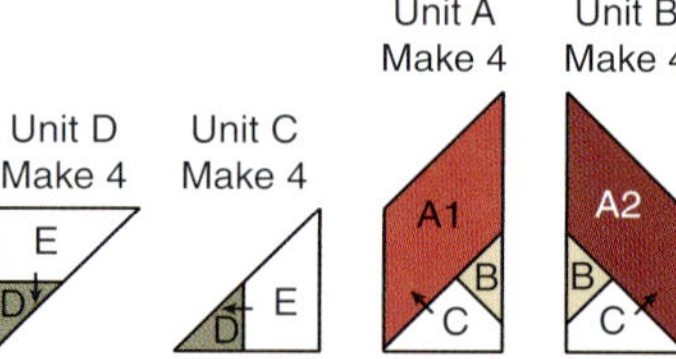


**Figure 1**

## Here's a Tip

*To ensure that all matching intersections in your Poinsettia block are easy to assemble, press the seams of each mirrored unit in opposite directions. This will ensure that all the pieces fit together perfectly.*

**3.** Refer to the Poinsettia block diagram and arrange the foundation units in pairs. Join the units in pairs; sew the pairs together to create a quarter-block (Figure 2). Join the quarter-blocks together in rows; join the rows to complete the Poinsettia block.

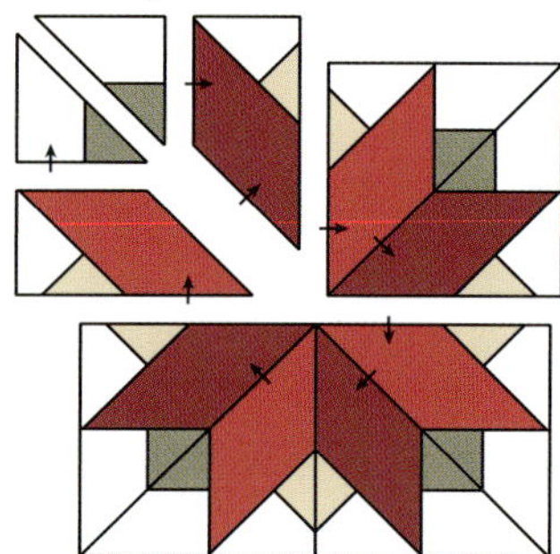

**Figure 2**

**4.** Refer to Raw-Edge Fusible Appliqué on page 46 and prepare the template for the poinsettia center using the pattern provided. Trace around the poinsettia center, cut apart and fuse to the wrong side of green #2. Cut out on pattern lines, remove paper backing and appliqué to the center of the Poinsettia block.

## Inspiration

*"Poinsettias evoke a feeling of winter to me. I wanted to design a project that would be quick and easy to make, but also have a bit of a challenge. The Poinsettia block in this quilt is perfect for giving you just the right amount of difficulty while still being achievable." —Debra Clutter*

## LOG CABIN BLOCKS

**1.** Sew an H rectangle to a G square (Figure 3). Make two.

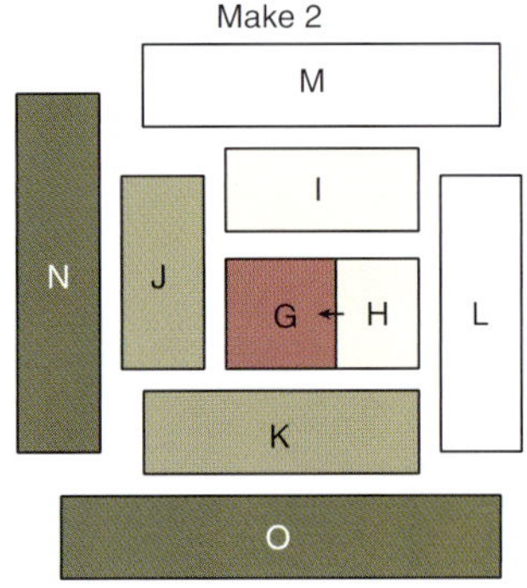


**Figure 3**

**2.** Refer to the Log Cabin block diagram and continue adding strips I–O to the step 1 unit in alphabetical order, working counter-clockwise, to complete two Log Cabin blocks. Press toward each new strip.

## FOUR-PATCH BLOCKS

**1.** Refer to Eight-at-a-Time Half-Square Triangles on page 8 to make 48 HST units using R and S squares (Figure 4). Trim HST units to 2½" square, if necessary. There will be four extra HST units; remove one HST from each of four different color combinations.

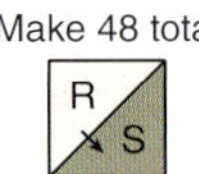


**Figure 4**

**2.** Refer to the Four-Patch block diagram and arrange two HST units and two T squares in two rows as shown, noting orientation of HST units. Sew units and squares together in rows; join the rows to complete the block. Make 20.

**3.** Refer to Figure 5 and sew one HST unit to a T square, noting orientation of the HST unit to make a two-patch unit. Make one of each variation shown for a total of four.

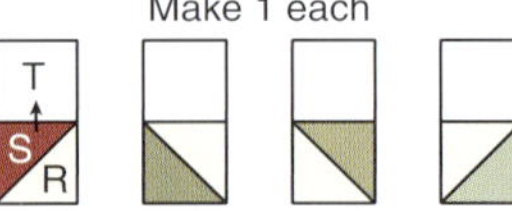


**Figure 5**

## COMPLETING THE RUNNER

Refer to the Assembly Diagram to complete runner top.

**1.** Arrange and sew together Log Cabin and Poinsettia blocks as shown. Remove the foundation papers from the Poinsettia block.

**2.** Sew the borders to the runner center in alphabetical order.

**3.** Arrange and sew together six Four-Patch blocks and one two-patch unit to make a long border. Make two.

**4.** In the same manner, sew together four Four-Patch blocks and one two-patch unit to make a short border. Make two.

**5.** Sew the borders to the runner center to complete the runner top.

**6.** From fabric scraps, cut 2½" strips and piece together 120" of binding.

**7.** Layer, baste, quilt as desired and bind referring to Quilting Basics. The photographed table runner was quilted with continuous curves and straight-line echo quilting. ■

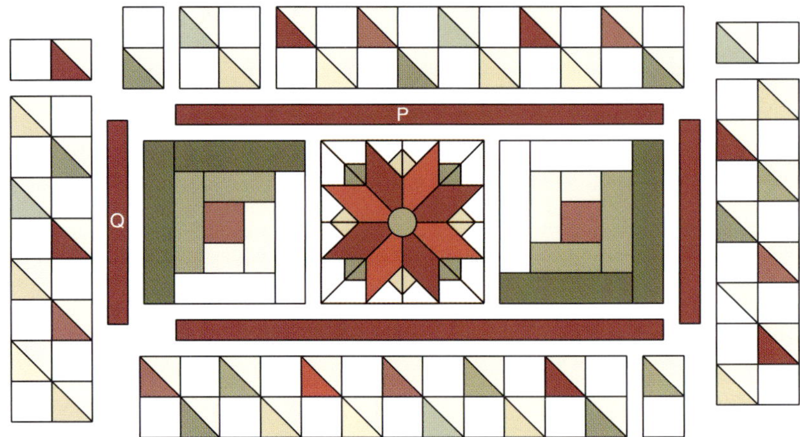


**Cozy Log Cabin Runner**
Assembly Diagram 18" x 34"

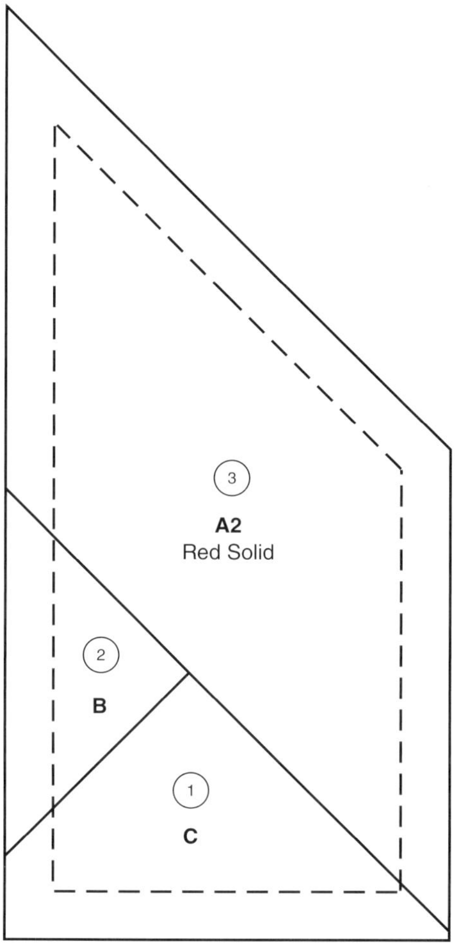

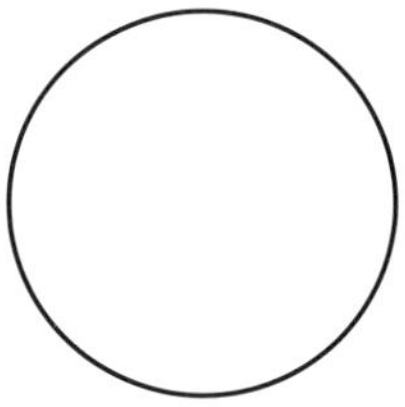

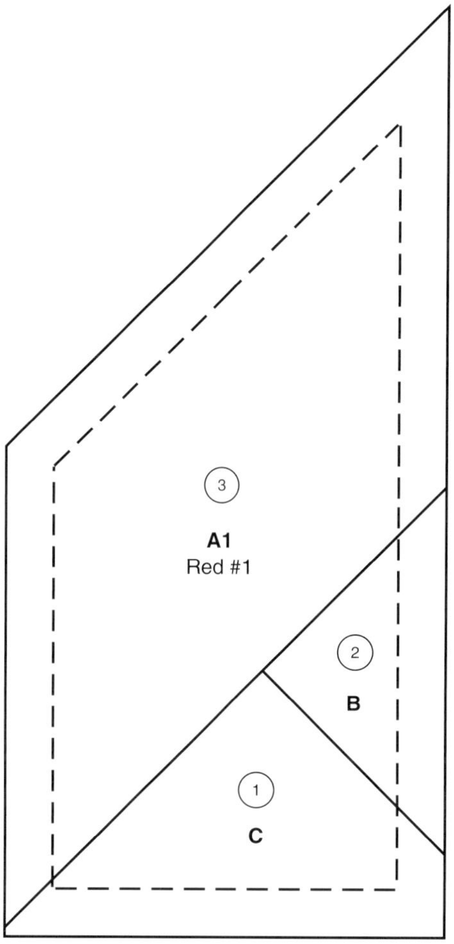

3
A2
Red Solid
2
B
1
C

**Cozy Log Cabin Runner**
Poinsettia Center
Cut as per instructions

3
A1
Red #1
2
B
1
C

**Cozy Log Cabin Runner**
Foundation A
Make 4

**Cozy Log Cabin Runner**
Foundation B
Make 4

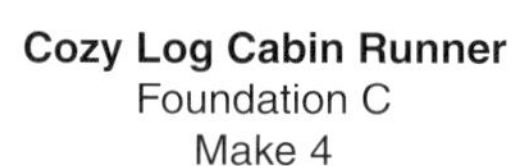

**Cozy Log Cabin Runner**
Foundation C
Make 4

2
D
1
E

2
D
1
E

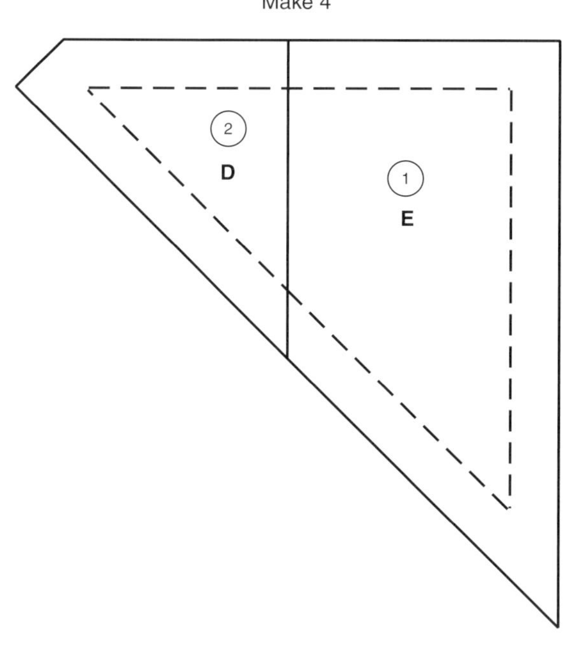

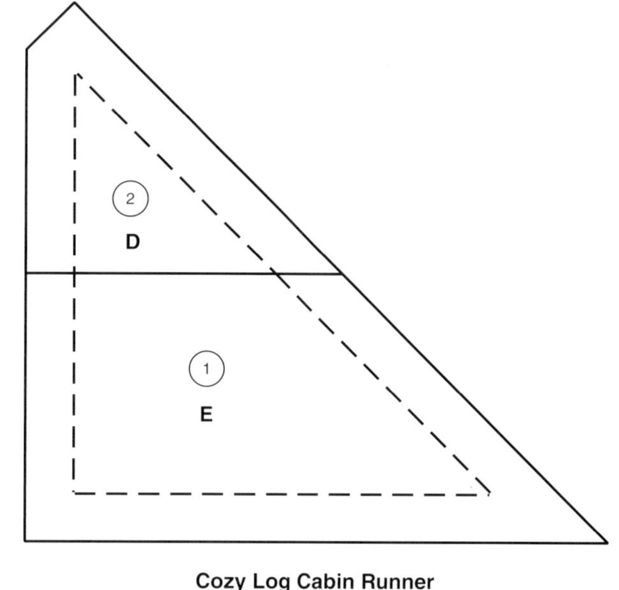

**Cozy Log Cabin Runner**
Foundation D
Make 4

# RAW-EDGE FUSIBLE APPLIQUÉ

One of the easiest ways to appliqué is the raw-edge fusible-web method. Individual pieces of paper-backed fusible web are fused to the wrong side of specified fabrics, cut out and then fused together in a motif or individually to a foundation fabric, where they are machine-stitched in place.

## Choosing Appliqué Fabrics

Depending on the appliqué, you may want to consider using batiks. Batik is a much tighter weave and, because of the manufacturing process, does not fray. If you are thinking about using regular quilting cottons, be sure to stitch your raw-edge appliqués with blanket/buttonhole stitches instead of a straight stitch.

## Cutting Appliqué Pieces

**1.** Fusible appliqué shapes should be reversed for this technique.

**2.** Trace the appliqué shapes onto the paper side of paper-backed fusible web. Leave at least ¼" between shapes. Cut out shapes leaving a margin around traced lines. ***Note:*** *If doing several identical appliqués, trace reversed shapes onto template material to make reusable templates for tracing shapes onto the fusible web.*

**3.** Follow manufacturer's instructions and fuse shapes to wrong side of fabric as indicated on pattern for color and number to cut.

**4.** Cut out appliqué shapes on traced lines. Remove paper backing from shapes.

**5.** Again following fusible web manufacturer's instructions, arrange and fuse pieces to quilt referring to quilt pattern. Or fuse together shapes on top of an appliqué ironing mat to make an appliqué motif that can then be fused to the quilt.

## Stitching Appliqué Edges

Machine-stitch appliqué edges to secure the appliqués in place and help finish the raw edges with matching or invisible thread (Photo A). ***Note:*** *To show stitching, all samples have been stitched with contrasting thread.*

**Photo A**

Invisible thread can be used to stitch appliqués down when using the blanket or straight stitches. Do not use it for the satin stitch. Definitely practice with invisible thread before using it on your quilt; it can sometimes be difficult to work with.

A short, narrow buttonhole or blanket stitch is most commonly used (Photo B). Your machine manual may also refer to this as an appliqué stitch. Be sure to stitch next to the appliqué edge with the stitch catching the appliqué.

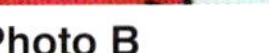
**Photo B**

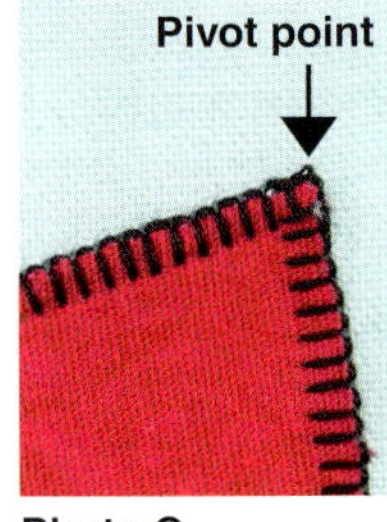

**Photo C**

Practice turning inside and outside corners on scrap fabric before stitching appliqué pieces. Learn how your machine stitches so that you can make the pivot points smooth (Photo C).

**1.** To stitch outer corners, stitch to the edge of the corner and stop with needle in the fabric at the corner point. Pivot to the next side of the corner and continue to sew (Photo D). You will get a box on an outside corner.

**Photo D**

**2.** To stitch inner corners, pivot at the inner point with needle in fabric (Photo E). You will see a Y shape in the corner.

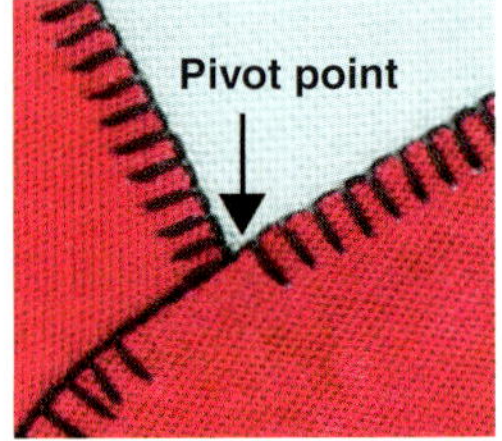

**Photo E**

**3.** You can also use a machine straight stitch. Turn corners in the same manner, stitching to the corners and pivoting with needle in down position (Photos F and G).

**Photo F**

**Photo G**

## General Appliqué Tips

**1.** Use a light- to medium-weight stabilizer behind an appliqué to keep the fabric from puckering during machine stitching (Photo H).

**Photo H**

**2.** To reduce the stiffness of a finished appliqué, cut out the center of the fusible web shape, leaving ¼"–½" inside the pattern line. This gives a border of adhesive to fuse to the background and leaves the center soft and easy to quilt.

**3.** If an appliqué fabric is so light colored or thin that the background fabric shows through, fuse a lightweight interfacing to the wrong side of the fabric. You can also fuse a piece of the appliqué fabric to a matching piece, wrong sides together, and then apply the fusible web with a drawn pattern to one side. ●

# Quilting Basics

The following is a reference guide. For more information, consult a comprehensive quilting book.

### Quilt Backing & Batting

Cut your backing and batting 8" larger than the finished quilt-top size and 4" larger for quilts smaller than 50" square. ***Note:*** *Check with longarm quilter about their requirements, if applicable. For baby quilts not going to a longarm quilter 4"–6" overall may be sufficient.* If preparing the backing from standard-width fabrics, remove the selvages and sew two or three lengths together; press seams open. If using 108"-wide fabric, trim to size on the straight grain of the fabric. Prepare batting the same size as your backing.

### Quilting

**1.** Press quilt top on both sides and trim all loose threads. ***Note:*** *If you are sending your quilt to a longarm quilter, contact them for specifics about preparing your quilt for quilting.*

**2.** Mark quilting design on quilt top. Make a quilt sandwich by layering the backing right side down, batting and quilt top centered right side up on flat surface and smooth out. Baste layers together using pins, thread basting or spray basting to hold. ***Note:*** *Tape or pin backing to surface to hold taut while layering and avoid puckers.*

**3.** Quilt as desired by hand or machine. Remove pins or basting as you quilt.

**4.** Trim batting and backing edges even with raw edges of quilt top.

### Binding the Quilt

**1.** Join binding strips on short ends with diagonal seams to make one long strip; trim seams to ¼" and press seams open (Figure 1).

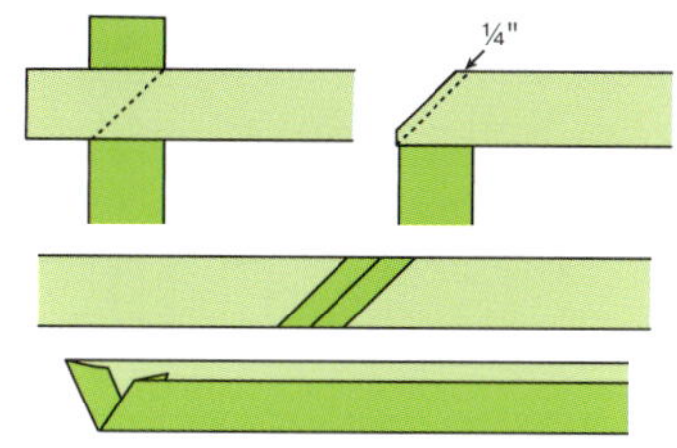


**Figure 1**

**2.** Fold ½" of one short end to wrong side and press. Fold the binding strip in half with wrong sides together along length, again referring to Figure 1; press.

**3.** Starting about 3" from the folded short end, sew binding to quilt top edges, matching raw edges and using a ¼" seam. Stop stitching ¼" from corner and backstitch (Figure 2).

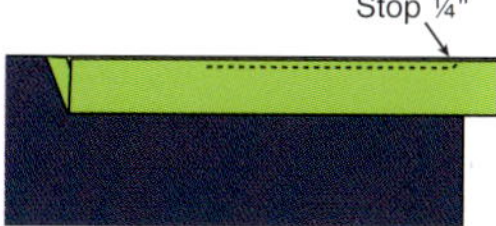


**Figure 2**

**4.** Fold binding up at a 45-degree angle to seam and then down even with quilt edges, forming a pleat at corner (Figure 3).

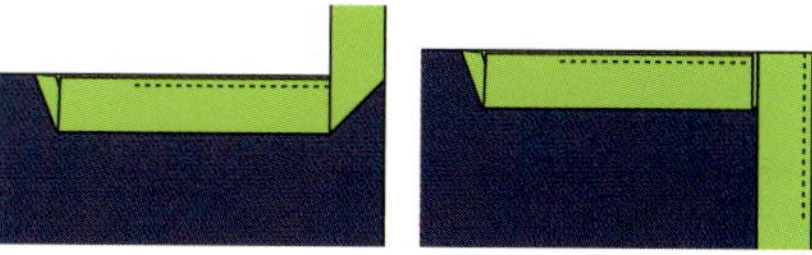

**Figure 3**

**5.** Resume stitching from corner edge as shown in Figure 3, down quilt side, backstitching ¼" from next corner. Repeat, mitering all corners, stitching to within 3" of starting point.

**6.** Trim binding, leaving enough length to tuck inside starting end and complete stitching (Figure 4).

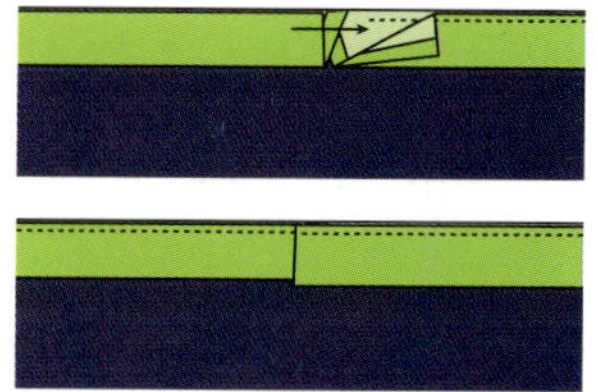

**Figure 4**

**7.** If stitching binding by hand, machine-sew binding to the front of the quilt and fold to the back before stitching. If stitching by machine, machine-sew binding to back of the quilt and fold to the front before stitching.

# SPECIAL THANKS

## Please join us in thanking the talented designers whose work is featured in this collection.

**Debra Clutter**
Cozy Log Cabin Runner, 41

**Megan Dahlinger**
Christmas Puzzle, 17

**Jen Daly**
Log Cabin Christmas, 19

**Preeti Harris**
Joyful, 13

**Joy Heimark**
Festive Yuletide, 35

**Jill Metzger**
Mistletoe & Mint, 5

**Jenny Kae Parks**
Christmas Mosaic, 23

**Kim Ratchford**
Sleigh Ride, 28

**Mercedes Rose**
Christmas Dishes, 2

# SUPPLIES

## We would like to thank the following manufacturers who provided materials to our designers to make sample projects for this book.

**Christmas Dishes, page 2:** Fabrics from the Shimmer Sparkle collection by Deborah Edwards for Northcott Fabrics.

**Mistletoe & Mint, page 5:** Fabrics from the Christmas Is In Town collection by Sandy Gervais and Confetti Cottons for Riley Blake Designs; Warm & Natural Cotton batting from The Warm Company.

**Joyful, page 13:** Thermore® batting by Hobbs Bonded Fibers.

**Log Cabin Christmas, page 19:** Fabrics from the Magical Winterland collection by Lisa Audit for Riley Blake Designs.

**Christmas Mosaic, page 23:** Fabrics from Cherrywood Fabrics.

**Sleigh Ride, page 28:** Fabrics from the Berry and Pine collection by Lella Boutique for Moda Fabrics; Dream 80/20 batting by Quilters Dream.

Published by Annie's Attic, 306 East Parr Road, Berne, IN 46711. Printed in USA.


ISBN: 979-8-89253-391-1

1 2 3 4 5 6 7 8 9